THE
ART
OF
STAR
WARS®

Illustration: Joe Heiner

THE
ART
OF

EDITED BY CAROL TITELMAN

**INCLUDING
THE COMPLETE SCRIPT
OF THE FILM
BY GEORGE LUCAS**

ART DIRECTION & DESIGN, MIKE SALISBURY
ASSISTANT EDITOR, VALERIE HOFFMAN
PHOTO RESEARCH, LINDSAY SMITH

A DEL REY® BOOK

BALLANTINE BOOKS · NEW YORK

Acknowledgments

We'd like to express warmest appreciation to
those who have worked for months to organize
these materials. Special thanks to Joel Coler, Fran Zell
and Denise Breton at Twentieth Century-Fox Film
Corporation, Jane Quinson at Ballantine Books,
Jane Bay, Deborah Call, and Robin Mitchell at
Lucasfilm.

Library of Congress Catalog Card Number: 78-31161

ISBN 0-345-39202-7

Cover designed by Michaelis/Carpelis Design Associates
Cover illustration by Ralph McQuarrie
Title page illustration copyright © 1979 Black Falcon Ltd.

Manufactured in the United States of America
First Edition: November 1979
Reissued: October 1994
10 9 8 7 6 5 4 3 2 1

FOREWORD

The Art of Star Wars contains an abundance of sketches and paintings that recreate the imaginative process that went into the making of Star Wars.

For the reader's convenience, the book is divided into three sections. The first contains the script, annotated by hundreds of visuals, many of which demonstrate the changing plotline and evolution of the characters. The second chapter consists of numerous examples of poster art, including advertising posters that were developed to present the film to the public in the United States as well as abroad. Finally, we devote the last section of *The Art of Star Wars* to the interpretations of the film by professional comic artists and cartoonists and the young fans who sustain the Star Wars theme.

SECTION ONE 1 THE SCRIPT

S T A R   W A R S

====

EPISODE

IV

A NEW HOPE

FROM THE

JOURNAL OF THE WHILLS

BY

GEORGE LUCAS

REVISED FOURTH DRAFT
JANUARY 15, 1976

LUCASFILM LTD.

Storyboards: Gary Myers, Paul
Huston, Steve Gawley, Ronnie
Shepherd; under the direction of
Joe Johnston

 long time ago, in a galaxy far, far, away…

A vast sea of stars serves as the backdrop for the main title. War drums echo through the heavens as a rollup slowly crawls into infinity.

It is a period of civil war. Rebel spaceships, striking from a hidden base, have won their first victory against the evil Galactic Empire.

During the battle, Rebel spies managed to steal secret plans to the Empire's ultimate weapon, the Death Star, an armored space station with enough power to destroy an entire planet.

Pursued by the Empire's sinister agents, Princess Leia races home aboard her starship, custodian of the stolen plans that can save her people and restore freedom to the galaxy…

Above: Sketches of Artoo-Detoo, Ralph McQuarrie; below: storyboard, Alex Tavoularis

CENE 1 - FRAME 1 -
FADE IN - A VAST SEA OF STARS - ROLL TITLES,
BOTTOM TO TOP, CONVERGE @ INF.

The awesome yellow planet of Tatooine emerges from a total eclipse, her two moons glowing against the darkness. A tiny silver spacecraft, a Rebel Blockade Runner firing lasers from the back of the ship, races through space. It is pursued by a giant Imperial starship. Hundreds of deadly laserbolts streak from the Imperial Stardestroyer, causing the main solar fin of the Rebel craft to disintegrate.

INTERIOR: REBEL BLOCKADE RUNNER—
MAIN PASSAGEWAY.

An explosion rocks the ship as two robots, Artoo-Detoo (R2-D2) and See-Threepio (C-3PO) struggle to make their way through the shaking, bouncing passageway. Both robots are old and battered. Artoo is a short, claw-armed tripod. His face is a mass of computer lights surrounding a radar eye. Threepio, on the other hand, is a tall, slender robot of human proportions. He has a gleaming bronze-like metallic surface of an Art Deco design.

Another blast shakes them as they struggle along their way.

THREEPIO: Did you hear that? They've shut down the main reactor. We'll be destroyed for sure. This is madness!

Rebel troopers rush past the robots and take up positions in the main passageway. They aim their weapons toward the door.

THREEPIO: We're doomed!

The little R2 unit makes a series of electronic sounds that only another robot could understand.

THREEPIO: There'll be no escape for the Princess this time.

Artoo continues making beeping sounds. Tension mounts as loud metallic latches clank and the screams of heavy equipment are heard moving around the outside hull of the ship.

THREEPIO: What's that?

EXTERIOR: SPACECRAFT IN SPACE.

The Imperial craft has easily overtaken the Rebel Blockade Runner. The smaller Rebel ship is being drawn into the underside dock of the giant Imperial starship.

INTERIOR: REBEL BLOCKADE RUNNER.

The nervous Rebel troopers aim their weapons. Suddenly a tremendous blast opens up a hole in the main passageway and a score of fearsome armored spacesuited stormtroopers make their way into the smoke-filled corridor.

In a few minutes the entire passageway is ablaze with laserfire. The deadly bolts ricochet in wild random patterns creating huge explosions. Stormtroopers scatter and duck behind storage lockers. Laserbolts hit several Rebel soldiers who scream and stagger through the smoke, holding shattered arms and faces.

An explosion hits near the robots.

THREEPIO: I should have known better than to trust the logic of a half-sized thermocapsulary dehousing assister...

Artoo counters with an angry rebuttal as the battle rages around the two hapless robots.

EXTERIOR: TATOOINE—DESERT WASTELAND—DAY.

A death-white wasteland stretches from horizon to horizon. The tremendous heat of two huge twin suns settles on a lone figure, Luke Skywalker, a farm boy with heroic aspirations who looks much younger than his eighteen years. His shaggy hair and baggy tunic give him the air of a simple but lovable lad with a prize-winning smile.

A light wind whips at him as he adjusts several valves on a large battered moisture vaporator which sticks out of the desert floor much like an oil pipe with valves. He is aided by a beatup tread-robot with six claw arms. The little robot appears to be barely functioning and moves with jerky motions. A bright sparkle in the morning sky catches Luke's eye and he instinctively grabs a pair of electrobinoculars from his utility belt. He stands transfixed for a few moments studying the heavens, then dashes toward his dented, crudely repaired Landspeeder (an auto-like transport that travels a few feet above the ground on a magnetic field). He motions for the tiny robot to follow him.

LUKE: Hurry up! Come with me! What are you waiting for?! Get in gear!

The robot scoots around in a tight circle, stops short, and smoke begins to pour out of every joint. Luke throws his arms up in disgust. Exasperated, the young farm boy jumps into his Landspeeder leaving the smoldering robot to hum madly.

Above: Sketches of Luke, Ralph McQuarrie; below: storyboard, Alex Tavoularis

Opposite page: Matte painting of Tatooine, Ralph McQuarrie

Early sketches of Artoo-Detoo,
Ralph McQuarrie

Photograph of Artoo-Detoo,
Bob Seidemann

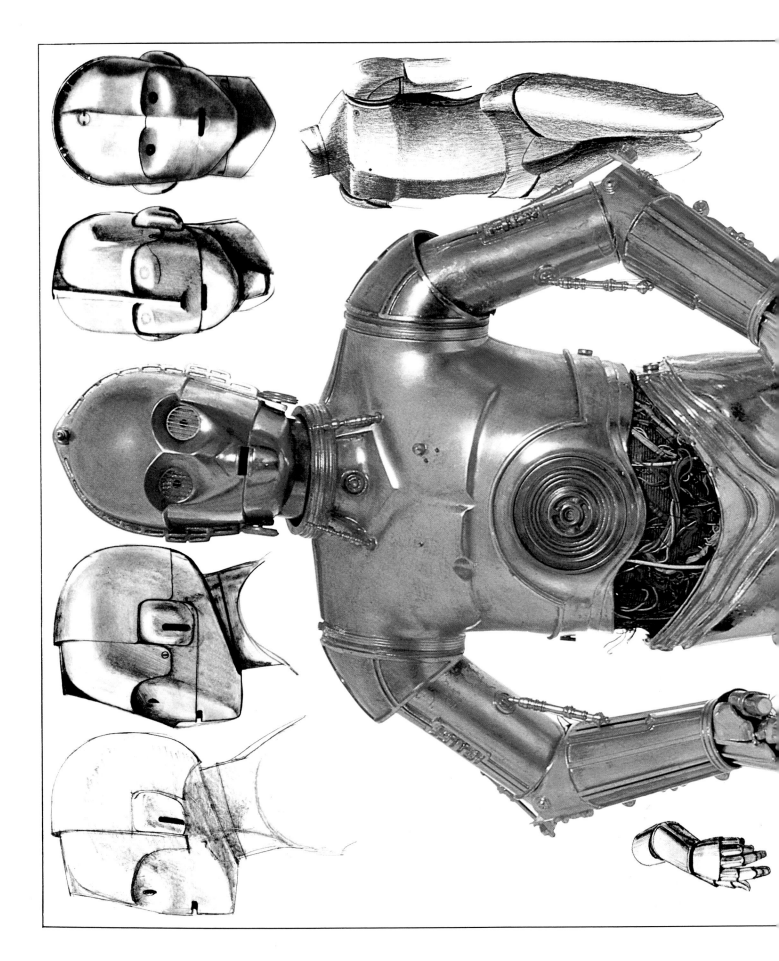

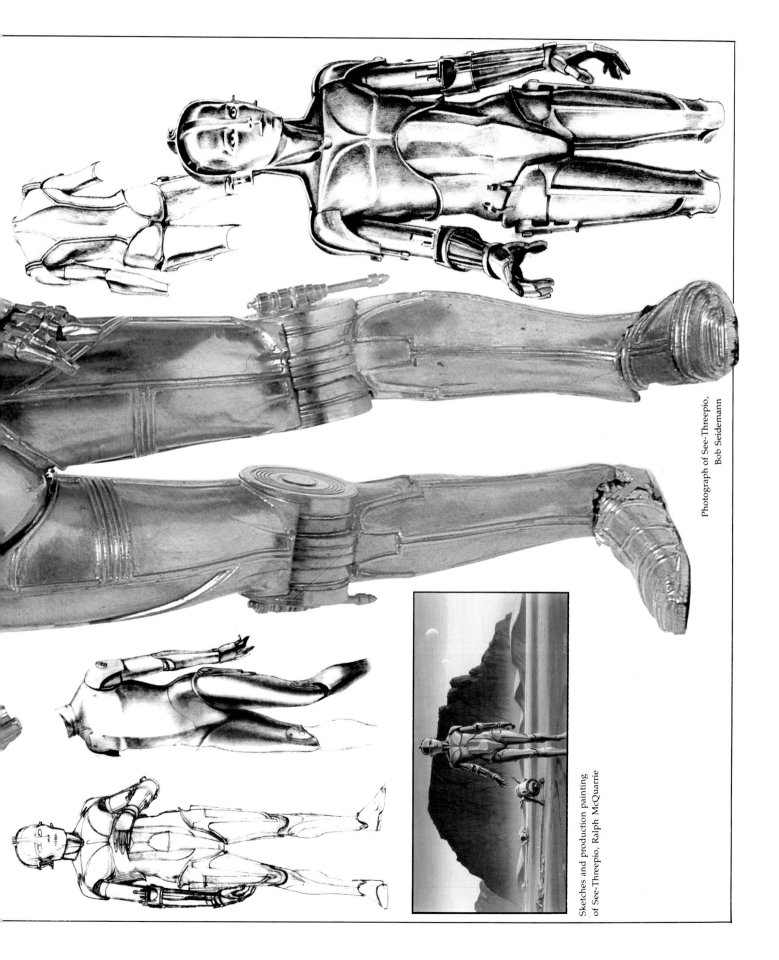

Photograph of See-Threepio,
Bob Seidemann

Sketches and production painting
of See-Threepio, Ralph McQuarrie

Luke Skywalker
Below: Photograph,
Bob Seidemann:
right: sketch, Ralph McQuarrie

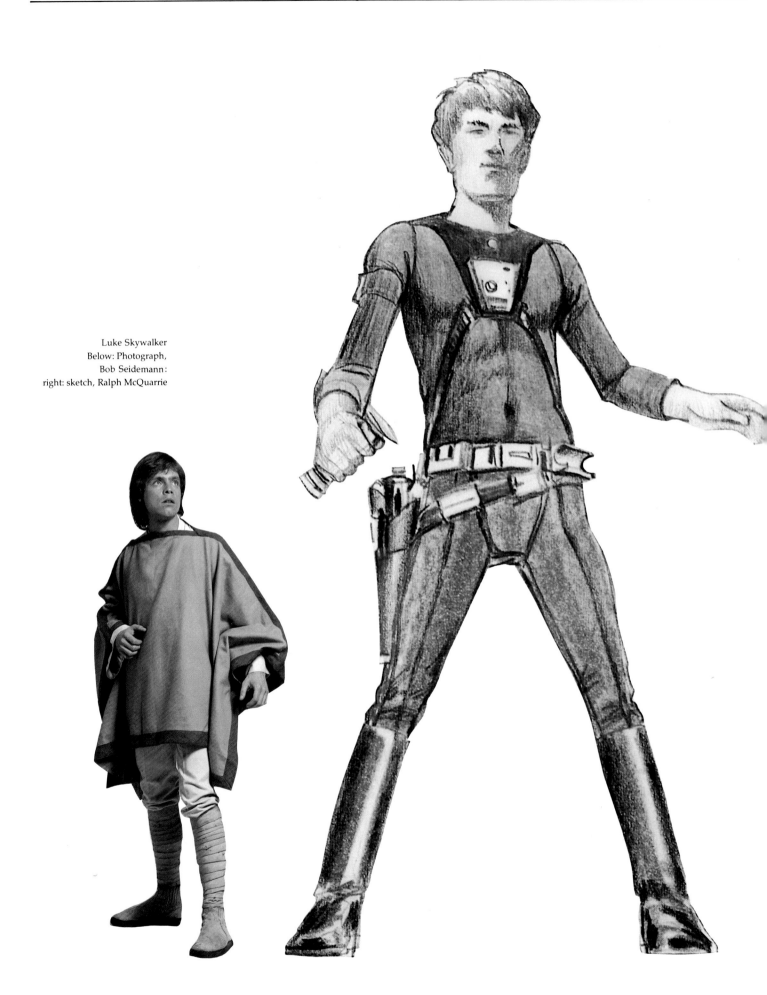

Left: Sketch, Ralph McQuarrie;
photographs, Bob Seidemann;
below: sketch, John Mollo

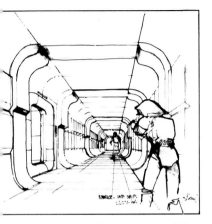

Above: Sketch, John Barry; below: photograph of Rebel Blockade Runner model, Richard Edlund

INTERIOR: REBEL BLOCKADE RUNNER—
MAIN HALLWAY

The awesome, seven-foot-tall Dark Lord of The Sith makes his way into the blinding light of the main passageway. This is Darth Vader, right hand of the Emperor. His face is obscured by his flowing black robes and grotesque breath mask, which stands out next to the fascist white armored suits of the Imperial stormtroopers. Everyone instinctively backs away from the imposing warrior and a deathly quiet sweeps through the Rebel troops. Several of the Rebel troops break and run in a frenzied panic.

INTERIOR: REBEL BLOCKADE RUNNER

A woman's hand puts a card into an opening in Artoo's dome. Artoo makes beeping sounds.

INTERIOR: REBEL BLOCKADE RUNNER

Threepio stands in a hallway, somewhat bewildered. Artoo is nowhere in sight. The pitiful screams of the doomed Rebel soldiers can be heard in the distance.
THREEPIO: Artoo! Artoo-Detoo, where are you?
A familiar clanking sound attracts Threepio's attention and he spots little Artoo at the end of the hallway in a smoke-filled alcove. A beautiful young girl (about sixteen years old) stands in front of Artoo. Surreal and out of place, dreamlike and half hidden in the smoke, she finishes adjusting something on Artoo's computer face, then watches as the little robot joins his companion.
THREEPIO: At last! Where have you been?
Stormtroopers can be heard battling in the distance.
THREEPIO: They're heading in this direction. What

are we going to do? We'll be sent to the spice mine of Kessel or smashed into who-knows-what!
Artoo scoots past his bronze friend and races down the subhallway. Threepio chases after him.
THREEPIO: Wait a minute, where are you going?
Artoo responds with electronics beeps.

INTERIOR: REBEL BLOCKADE RUNNER—CORRIDOR

The evil Darth Vader stands amid the broken and twisted bodies of his foes. He grabs a wounded Rebel Officer by the neck as an Imperial Officer rushes up to the Dark Lord.
IMPERIAL OFFICER: The Death Star plans are not in the main computer.
Vader squeezes the neck of the Rebel Officer, who struggles in vain.
VADER: Where are those transmissions you intercepted?
Vader lifts the Rebel off his feet by his throat.
VADER: What have you done with those plans?
REBEL OFFICER: We intercepted no transmissions. Aaah....This is a consular ship. We're on a diplomatic mission.
VADER: If this is a consular ship...where's the Ambassador?
The Rebel refuses to speak but eventually cries out as the Dark Lord begins to squeeze the officer's throat, creating a gruesome snapping and choking, until the soldier goes limp. Vader tosses the dead soldier against the wall and turns to his troops.
VADER: Commander, tear this ship apart until you've found those plans and bring me the Ambassador. I want her alive!
The stormtroopers scurry into the subhallways.

INTERIOR: REBEL BLOCKADE RUNNER—SUBHALLWAY

The lovely young girl huddles in a small alcove as the stormtroopers search through the ship. She is Princess Leia Organa, a member of the Alderaan Senate. The fear in her eyes slowly gives way to anger as the muted crushing sounds of the approaching stormtroopers grow louder. One of the troopers spots her.
TROOPER: There she is! Set for stun!

Leia steps from her hiding place and blasts a trooper with her laser pistol. She starts to run but is felled by a paralyzing ray. The troopers inspect her inert body.
TROOPER: She'll be all right. Inform Lord Vader we have a prisoner.

INTERIOR: REBEL BLOCKADE RUNNER—SUBHALLWAY

Artoo stops before the small hatch of an emergency lifepod. He snaps the seal on the main latch and a red warning light begins to flash. The stubby astro-robot works his way into the cramped four-man pod.
THREEPIO: Hey, you're not permitted in there. It's restricted. You'll be deactivated for sure.

Artoo beeps something to him.
THREEPIO: Don't call me a mindless philosopher, you overweight glob of grease! Now come out before somebody sees you.

Artoo whistles something at his reluctant friend regarding the mission he is about to perform.
THREEPIO: Secret mission? What plans? What are you talking about? I'm not getting in there!

Artoo isn't happy with Threepio's stubbornness, and he beeps and twangs angrily.

A new explosion, this time very close, sends dust and debris through the narrow subhallway. Flames lick at Threepio and, after a flurry of electronic swearing from Artoo, the lanky robot jumps into the lifepod.
THREEPIO: I'm going to regret this.

EXTERIOR: REBEL BLOCKADE RUNNER

The safety door snaps shut, and with the thunder of exploding latches the tiny lifepod ejects from the disabled ship.

INTERIOR: IMPERIAL STARDESTROYER

On the main viewscreen, the lifepod carrying the two terrified robots speeds away from the stricken Rebel spacecraft.
CHIEF PILOT: There goes another one.
CAPTAIN: Hold your fire. There are no life forms. It must have been short-circuited.

INTERIOR: LIFEPOD

Artoo and Threepio look out at the receding Imperial starship. Stars circle as the pod rotates through the galaxy.
THREEPIO: That's funny, the damage doesn't look as bad from out here.
Artoo beeps an assuring response.
THREEPIO: Are you sure this thing is safe?

EXTERIOR: TATOOINE—ANCHORHEAD SETTLEMENT—POWER STATION—DAY

Heat waves radiate from the dozen or so bleached white buildings. Luke pilots his Landspeeder through the dusty empty street of the tiny settlement. An old Woman runs to

Above: Early sketches of Imperial stormtrooper helmets, Ralph McQuarrie; left: photograph of Imperial stormtrooper, Bob Seidemann

Sketches of Darth Vader,
Ralph McQuarrie

Composite photograph of Darth
Vader, Bob Seideman; airbrushed
by Ralph McQuarrie

Costume Sketches of
Princess Leia

Above: John Mollo; right:
Ralph McQuarrie

Above: Ralph McQuarrie ; below: John Mollo

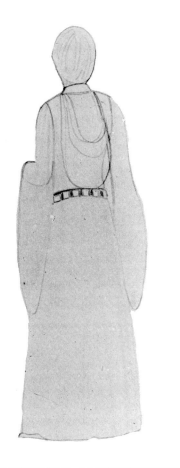

Above: John Mollo; left:
Ralph McQuarrie

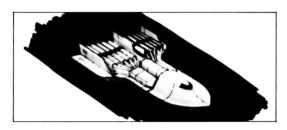

Opposite page: Composite photograph of Star Destroyer model; photograph, Richard Edlund; airbushing, Ralph McQuarrie; left: drawing, John Barry

get out of the way of the speeding vehicle, shaking her fist at Luke as he flies past.

WOMAN: I've told you kids to slow down!

Luke pulls up behind a low concrete service station that is all but covered by the shifting desert sands.

INTERIOR: POWER STATION—DAY

Luke bursts into the power station, waking The Fixer, a rugged mechanic and Camie, a sexy, disheveled girl who has been asleep on his lap. They grumble as he races through the office, yelling wildly.

FIXER: Did I hear a young noise blast through here?

CAMIE: It was just Wormie on another rampage.

Luke bounces into a small room behind the office where Deak and Windy, two tough boys about the same age as Luke, are playing a computer pool-like game with Biggs, a burly, handsome boy a few years older than the rest. His flashy city attire is a sharp contrast to the loose-fitting tunics of the farm boys. A robot repairs some equipment in the background.

LUKE: Shape it up you guys!...Biggs?

Luke's surprise at the appearance of Biggs gives way to great joy and emotion. They give each other a great bear hug.

LUKE: I didn't know you were back! When did you get in?

BIGGS: Just now. I wanted to surprise you, hot shot. I thought you'd be here...certainly didn't expect you to be out working. (he laughs.)

LUKE: The Academy didn't change you much...but you're back so soon? Hey, what happened, didn't you get your commission?

Biggs has an air of cool that seems slightly phony.

BIGGS: Of course I got it. Signed aboard The Rand Ecliptic last week. First mate Biggs Darklighter at your service...(he salutes)...I just came back to say good-bye to all you unfortunate landlocked simpletons.

Everyone laughs. The dazzling spectacle of his dashing friend is almost too much for Luke, but suddenly he snaps out of it.

Left: Photograph of vaporators on location in Tunisia; below: drawing of vaporator, John Barry

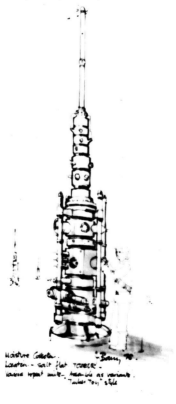

Above: Sketches of Camie, The Fixer, and Biggs; John Mollo

LUKE: I almost forgot. There's a battle going on! Right here in our system. Come and look!

DEAK: Not again! Forget it.

EXTERIOR: TATOOINE—ANCHORHEAD—SETTLEMENT—POWER STATION—DAY

The group stumbles out into the stifling desert sun. Camie and The Fixer complain and are forced to shade their eyes. Luke has his binoculars out scanning the heavens.

LUKE: There they are!

Biggs takes the binoculars from Luke as the others strain to see something with the naked eye. Through the binoculars Biggs sees two small silver specks.

BIGGS: That's no battle, hot shot... they're just sitting there! Probably a freighter-tanker refueling.

LUKE: But there was a lot of firing earlier...

Camie grabs the binoculars away banging them against the building in the process. Luke grabs them.

LUKE: Hey, easy with those...

CAMIE: Don't worry about it, Wormie.

The Fixer gives Luke a hard look and the young farm boy shrugs his shoulders in resignation.

FIXER: I keep telling you, the Rebellion is a long way from here. I doubt if the Empire would even fight to keep this system. Believe me Luke, this planet is a big hunk of nothing...

Luke agrees, although it's obvious he isn't sure why. The group stumbles back into the power station, grumbling about Luke's ineptitude.

INTERIOR: REBEL BLOCKADE RUNNER—HALLWAY

Princess Leia is led down a low-ceilinged hallway by a squad of armored stormtroopers. Her hands are bound and she is brutally shoved when she is unable to keep up with the briskly marching troops. They stop in a smoky hallway as Darth Vader emerges from the shadows. The sinister Dark Lord stares hard at the frail young senator, but she doesn't move.

LEIA: Lord Vader, I should have known. Only you could be so bold. The Imperial Senate will not sit still for this, when they hear you've attacked a diplomatic...

VADER: Don't play games with me, Your Highness. You weren't on any mercy mission this time. You passed directly through a restricted system. Several transmissions were beamed to this ship by Rebel spies. I want to know what happened to the plans they sent you.

LEIA: I don't know what you're talking about. I'm a member of the Imperial Senate on a diplomatic mission to Alderaan...

VADER: You're a part of the Rebel Alliance... and a traitor. Take her away!

Leia is marched away down the hallway and into the smoldering hole blasted in the side of the ship. An Imperial Commander turns to Vader.

COMMANDER: Holding her is dangerous. If word of this gets out, it could generate sympathy for the Rebellion in the senate.

Right: Sketches of Artoo-Detoo, Ralph McQuarrie

VADER: I have traced the Rebel spies to her. Now she is my only link to find their secret base!

COMMANDER: She'll die before she'll tell you anything.

VADER: Leave that to me. Send a distress signal and then inform the senate that all aboard were killed!

Another Imperial Officer approaches Vader and the Commander. They stop and snap to attention.

SECOND OFFICER: Lord Vader, the battle station plans are not aboard this ship! And no transmissions were made. An escape pod was jettisoned during the fighting, but no life forms were aboard.

Vader turns to the commander.

VADER: She must have hidden the plans in the escape pod. Send a detachment down to retrieve them. See to it personally, Commander. There'll be no one to stop us this time.

SECOND OFFICER: Yes, sir.

EXTERIOR: SPACE.

The Imperial Stardestroyer comes over the surface of the planet Tatooine.

EXTERIOR: TATOOINE—DESERT

Jundland, or "No Man's Land," where the rugged desert mesas meet the foreboding dune sea. The two helpless astro-robots kick up clouds of sand as they leave the lifepod and clumsily work their way across the desert wasteland. The lifepod in the distance rests half buried in the sand.

THREEPIO: How did we get into this mess? I really don't know how. We seem to be made to suffer. It's our lot in life.

Artoo answers with beeping sounds.

THREEPIO: I've got to rest before I fall apart. My joints are almost frozen.

Artoo continues to respond with beeping sounds.

THREEPIO: What a desolate place this is.

Suddenly Artoo whistles, makes a sharp right turn and starts off in the direction of the rocky desert mesas. Threepio stops and yells at him.

THREEPIO: Where are you going?

A stream of electronic noises pours forth from the small robot.

THREEPIO: Well, I'm not going that way. It's much too rocky. This way is much easier.

Artoo counters with a long whistle.

THREEPIO: What makes you think there are settlements over there?

Artoo continues to make beeping sounds.

THREEPIO: Don't get technical with me.

Artoo continues to make beeping sounds.

THREEPIO: What mission? What are you talking about? I've had just about enough of you! Go that way! You'll be malfunctioning within a day, you nearsighted scrap pile!

Threepio gives the little robot a kick and starts off in the direction of the vast dune sea.

THREEPIO: And don't let me catch you following me begging for help, because you won't get it.

Artoo's reply is a rather rude sound. He turns and trudges off in the direction of the towering mesas.

THREEPIO: No more adventures. I'm not going that way.

Artoo beeps to himself as he makes his way toward the distant mountains.

Left: Storyboards, Alex Tavoularis

EXTERIOR: TATOOINE—DUNE SEA

Threepio, hot and tired, struggles up over the ridge of a dune; only to find more dunes, which seem to go on for endless miles. He looks back in the direction of the now distant rock mesas.

THREEPIO: That malfunctioning little twerp. This is all his fault! He tricked me into going this way, but he'll do no better.

In a huff of anger and frustration, Threepio knocks the sand from his joints. His plight seems hopeless, when a glint of reflected light in the distance reveals an object moving toward him.

THREEPIO: Wait, what's that? A transport! I'm saved!

The bronze android waves frantically and yells at the approaching transport.

THREEPIO: Over here! Help! Please, help!

EXTERIOR: TATOOINE—ANCHORHEAD SETTLEMENT— POWER STATION—DAY

Luke and Biggs are walking and drinking a malt brew. Fixer and the others can be heard working inside.

LUKE: (Very animated)...so I cut off my power, shut down the afterburners and came in low on Deak's trail. I was so close I thought I was going to fry my instruments. As it was I busted up the Skyhopper pretty bad. Uncle Owen was pretty upset. He grounded me for the rest of the season. You should have been there...it was fantastic.

BIGGS: You ought to take it a little easy Luke. You may be the hottest bushpilot this side of Mos Eisley, but those little Skyhoppers are dangerous. Keep it up, and one day, whammo, you're going to be nothing more than a dark spot on the down side of a canyon wall.

LUKE: Look who's talking. Now that you've been around those giant starships you're beginning to sound like my uncle. You've gotten soft in the city...

BIGGS: I've missed you, kid.

LUKE: Well, things haven't been the same since you left, Biggs. It's been so...quiet.

Biggs looks around then leans close to Luke.

BIGGS: Luke, I didn't come back just to say good-bye...I shouldn't tell you this, but you're the only one I can trust...and if I don't come back, I want somebody to know.

Luke's eyes are wide with Biggs' seriousness and loyalty.

LUKE: What are you talking about?

BIGGS: I made some friends at the Academy. (he whispers)...when our frigate goes to one of the central systems, we're going to jump ship and join the Alliance...

Luke, amazed and stunned, is almost speechless.

LUKE: Join the Rebellion?! Are you kidding! How?

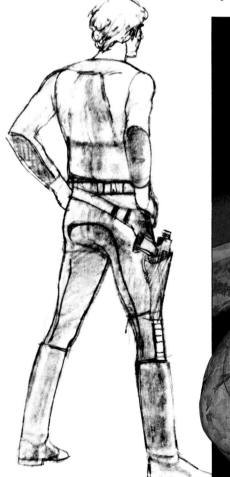

Below: Sketch of Luke, Ralph McQuarrie; right: photograph of Landspeeder, Richard Edlund

BIGGS: Quiet down will ya! You got a mouth bigger than a meteor crater!

LUKE: I'm sorry. I'm quiet. (he whispers) Listen how quiet I am. You can barely hear me...

Biggs shakes his head angrily and then continues.

BIGGS: My friend has a friend on Bestine who might help us make contact.

LUKE: You're crazy! You could wander around forever trying to find them.

BIGGS: I know it's a long shot, but if I don't find them I'll do what I can on my own...It's what we always talked about. Luke, I'm not going to wait for the Empire to draft me into service. The Rebellion is spreading and I want to be on the right side—the side I believe in.

LUKE: And I'm stuck here...

BIGGS: I thought you were going to the Academy next term. You'll get your chance to get off this rock.

LUKE: Not likely! I had to cancel my application. There has been a lot of unrest among the Sandpeople since you left...they've even raided the outskirts of Anchorhead.

BIGGS: Your uncle could hold off a whole colony of Sandpeople with one blaster.

LUKE: I know, but he's got enough vaporators going to make the place pay off. He needs me for just one more season. I can't leave him now.

BIGGS: I feel for you, Luke, you're going to have to learn what seems to be important or what really is important. What good is all your uncle's work if it's taken over by the Empire?...You know they're starting to nationalize commerce in the central systems...it won't be long before your uncle is merely a tenant, slaving for the greater glory of the Empire.

LUKE: It couldn't happen here. You said it yourself. The Empire won't bother with this rock.

BIGGS: Things always change.

LUKE: I wish I was going...Are you going to be around long?

BIGGS: No, I'm leaving in the morning...

LUKE: Then I guess I won't see you.

BIGGS: Maybe someday...I'll keep a lookout.

LUKE: Well, I'll be at the Academy next season... after that who knows. I won't be drafted into the Imperial Starfleet that's for sure...Take care of yourself, you'll always be the best friend I've got.

BIGGS: So long, Luke.

Biggs turns away from his old friend and heads back towards the power station.

EXTERIOR: TATOOINE—ROCK CANYON—
SUNSET

The gargantuan rock formations are shrouded in a strange foreboding mist and the ominous sounds of unearthly creatures fill the air. Artoo moves cautiously through the creepy rock canyon, inadvertently making a loud clicking

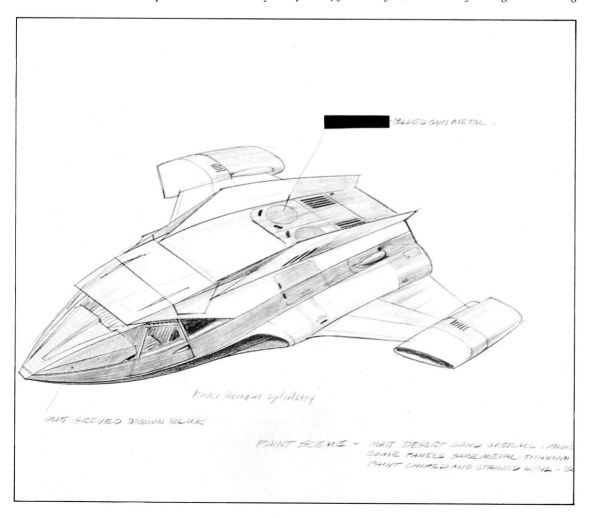

Left: Drawing of Landspeeder, Ralph McQuarrie

SHOT #

863-05

OPTICAL:

BACKGROUND:

PETER ELLEN

DESCRIPTION: JAWAS CARRY ARTOO TO S

DIALOGUE:

Right: Storyboard, Gary Myers,
Paul Huston, Steve Gawley,
Ronnie Shepherd; under direction
of Joe Johnston

P.P. #

PAGE #

FRAME COUNT:	BOARD #

RAWLER (DUSK)

ROTO:

Above: Photograph of Rock
Canyon location

noise as he goes. He hears a distant, hard, metallic sound and stops for a moment. Convinced he is alone, he continues on his way.

In the distance, a pebble tumbles down the steep canyon wall and a small dark figure darts into the shadows. A little further up the canyon a slight flicker of light reveals a pair of eyes in the dark recesses only a few feet from the narrow path.

The unsuspecting robot waddles along the rugged trail until suddenly, out of nowhere, a powerful magnetic ray shoots out of the rocks and engulfs him in an eerie glow. He manages one short electronic squeak before he topples over onto his back. His bright computer lights flicker off, then on, then off again. Out of the rocks scurry three Jawas, no taller than Artoo. They holster strange and complex weapons as they cautiously approach the robot. They wear grubby cloaks and their faces are shrouded so that only their glowing yellow eyes can be seen. They hiss and make odd guttural sounds as they heave the heavy robot onto their shoulders and carry him off down the trail.

EXTERIOR: TATOOINE—ROCK CANYON—
SANDCRAWLER—SUNSET

The eight Jawas carry Artoo out of the canyon to a huge tank-like vehicle the size of a four-story house. They weld a small disk on the side of Artoo and then put him under a large tube on the side of the vehicle and the little robot is sucked into the giant machine.

The filthy little Jawas scurry like rats up small ladders and enter the main cabin of the behemoth transport.

INTERIOR: SANDCRAWLER—HOLD AREA

It is dim inside the hold area of the Sandcrawler. Artoo switches on a small floodlight on his forehead and stumbles around the scrap heap. The narrow beam swings across rusty metal rocket parts and an array of grotesquely twisted and maimed astro-robots. He lets out a pathetic electronic whimper and stumbles off toward what appears to be a door at the end of the chamber.

INTERIOR: SANDCRAWLER—PRISON AREA

Artoo enters a wide room with a four-foot ceiling. In the middle of the scrap heap sit a dozen or so robots of various shapes and sizes. Some are engaged in electronic conversation, while others simply mill about. A voice of recognition calls out from the gloom.
THREEPIO: Artoo—Detoo! It's you! It's you!
A battered Threepio scrambles up to Artoo and embraces him.

EXTERIOR: TATOOINE—ROCK CANYON—
SANDCRAWLER—SUNSET

The enormous Sandcrawler lumbers off toward the magnificent twin suns, which are slowly setting over a distant mountain ridge.

EXTERIOR: TATOOINE—DESERT—DAY

Four Imperial stormtroopers mill about in front of the half-buried lifepod that brought Artoo and Threepio to Tatooine. A trooper yells to an officer some distance away.
FIRST TROOPER: Someone was in the pod. The tracks go off in this direction.
A Second Trooper picks a small bit of metal out of the sand and gives it to the first trooper.
SECOND TROOPER: Look, sir—droids.

EXTERIOR: TATOOINE—DUNES

The Sandcrawler moves slowly down a great sand dune.

INTERIOR: SANDCRAWLER

Threepio and Artoo noisily bounce along inside the cramped prison chamber. Artoo appears to be shut off.
THREEPIO: Wake up! Wake up!
Suddenly the shaking and bouncing of the Sandcrawler stops, creating quite a commotion among the mechanical men. Threepio's fist bangs the head of Artoo whose computer lights pop on as he begins beeping. At the far end of the long chamber a hatch opens, filling the chamber with blinding white light. A dozen or so Jawas make their way through the odd assortment of robots.
THREEPIO: We're doomed.
A Jawa starts moving toward them.
THREEPIO: Do you think they'll melt us down?
Artoo responds, making beeping sounds.
THREEPIO: Don't shoot! Don't shoot! Will this never end?

EXTERIOR: TATOOINE—DESERT—LARS
HOMESTEAD—AFTERNOON

The Jawas mutter gibberish as they busily line up their battered captives, including Artoo and Threepio, in front of the enormous Sandcrawler, which is parked beside a small homestead consisting of three large holes in the ground surrounded by several tall moisture vaporators and one small adobe block house.

The Jawas scurry around fussing over the robots, straightening them up or brushing some dust from a dented metallic elbow. The shrouded little creatures smell horribly, attracting small insects to the dark areas where their mouths and nostrils should be.

Out of the shadows of a dingy side-building limps Owen Lars, a large burly man in his mid-fifties. His reddish eyes are sunken in a dust-covered face. As the farmer carefully inspects each of the robots, he is closely followed by his slump-shouldered nephew, Luke Sky-walker. One of the vile little Jawas walks ahead of the farmer spouting an animated sales pitch in a queer, unintelligible language.

A voice calls out from one of the huge holes that form the homestead. Luke goes over to the edge and sees his Aunt Beru standing in the main courtyard.

BERU: Luke, tell Owen that if he gets a translator to be sure it speaks Bocce.

LUKE: It looks like we don't have much of a choice but I'll remind him.

Luke returns to his uncle as they look over the equipment for sale with the Jawa leader.

OWEN: I have no need for a protocol droid.

THREEPIO: (quickly) Sir—not in an environment such as this—that's why I've also been programmed for over thirty secondary functions that...

OWEN: What I really need is a droid that understands the binary language of moisture vaporators.

THREEPIO: Vaporators! Sir—My first job was programming binary load lifters...very similar to your vaporators. You could say...

OWEN: Do you speak Bocce?

THREEPIO: Of course I can, sir. It's like a second language for me...I'm as fluent in Bocce...

OWEN: All right; shut up! (turning to Jawa) I'll take this one.

THREEPIO: Shutting up, sir.

OWEN: Luke, take these two over to the garage, will you? I want you to have both of them cleaned up before dinner.

LUKE: But I was going into Toshi Station to pick up some power converters...

OWEN: You can waste time with your friends when your chores are done. Now come on, get to it!

LUKE: All right, come on! And the red one, come on. Well, come on, Red, let's go.

As the Jawas start to lead the three remaining robots back into the Sandcrawler, Artoo lets out a pathetic little beep and starts after his old friend Threepio. He is restrained by a slimy Jawa, who zaps him with a control box.

Owen is negotiating with the head Jawa. Luke and the two robots start for the garage when a plate pops off the head of the red astro-droid, throwing parts all over the ground. He adjusts the astro-droid's head plate and it sparks wildly.

LUKE: Uncle Owen...

OWEN: Yeah?

LUKE: This R2 unit has a bad motivator. Look!

OWEN: (to the head Jawa)
Hey, what're you trying to push on us?

The Jawa goes into a loud spiel. Meanwhile, Artoo has sneaked out of line and is moving up and down trying to attract attention. He lets out with a low whistle. Threepio taps Luke on the shoulder.

THREEPIO: (pointing to Artoo) Excuse me, sir, but that R2 unit is in prime condition. A real bargain.

LUKE: Uncle Owen...

OWEN: Yeah?

LUKE: What about that one?

OWEN: (to Jawa) What about that blue one? We'll take that one.

With a little reluctance the scruffy dwarf trades the damaged astro-robot for Artoo.

LUKE: Yeah, take this away.

THREEPIO: Uh, I'm quite sure you'll be very pleased with that one, sir. He really is in first-class condi-

tion. I've worked with him before. Here he comes.

Owen pays off the whining Jawa as Luke and the two robots trudge off toward a grimy homestead entry.

LUKE: Okay, let's go.

THREEPIO: (to Artoo) Now, don't forget this! Why I should stick my neck out for you is quite beyond my capacity!

Left: Thumbnail sketch for production painting, Ralph McQuarrie

Below: Production sketches of Lars homestead, John Barry; photograph of Lars homestead set in Tunisia

Left: Sketch of Tusken Raider,
John Mollo; center: photographs
of Jawa and Tusken Raider, Bob
Seidemann ; right: sketches of Jawa
and Tusken Raider, John Mollo

Top: Matte painting of
Sandcrawler, Ralph McQuarrie

Bottom: Photograph of
Sandcrawler model,
Richard Edlund

Left: Photograph of Sandcrawler
at Lars homestead set, John Jay

Above: Photograph of garage area at Lars homestead, John Jay; right: photograph through doorway of garage, John Jay

INTERIOR: LARS HOMESTEAD—GARAGE AREA—LATE AFTERNOON

The garage is cluttered and worn, but a friendly peaceful atmosphere permeates the low grey chamber. Threepio lowers himself into a large tub filled with warm oil. Near the battered Landspeeder little Artoo rests on a large battery with a cord attached to his face.

THREEPIO: Thank the maker! This oil bath is going to feel so good. I've got such a bad case of dust contamination, I can barely move!

Artoo beeps a muffled reply. Luke seems to be lost in thought as he runs his hand over the damaged fin of a small two-man Skyhopper spaceship resting in a low hangar off the garage. Finally Luke's frustrations get the better of him and he slams a wrench across the workbench.

LUKE: It just isn't fair. Oh, Biggs is right. I'm never gonna get out of here!

THREEPIO: Is there anything I might do to help?

Luke glances at the battered robot. A bit of his anger drains and a tiny smile creeps across his face.

LUKE: Well, not unless you can alter time, speed up the harvest, or teleport me off this rock!

THREEPIO: I don't think so, sir. I'm only a droid and not very knowledgeable about such things. Not on this planet, anyway. As a matter of fact, I'm not even sure which planet I'm on.

LUKE: Well, if there's a bright center to the universe, you're on the planet that it's farthest from.

THREEPIO: I see, sir.

LUKE: Uh, you can call me Luke.

THREEPIO: I see, Sir Luke.

LUKE: (laughing) Just Luke.

THREEPIO: And I am See-Threepio, human-cyborg relations, and this is my counterpart, Artoo-Detoo.

LUKE: Hello.

Artoo beeps in response. Luke unplugs Artoo and begins to scrape several connectors on the robot's head with a chrome pick. Threepio climbs out of the oil tub and begins wiping oil from his bronze body.

LUKE: You got a lot of carbon scoring here. It looks like you boys have seen a lot of action.

THREEPIO: With all we've been through, sometimes I'm amazed we're in as good condition as we are, what with the Rebellion and all.

Luke sparks to life at the mention of the Rebellion.

LUKE: You know of the Rebellion against the Empire?

THREEPIO: That's how we came to be in your service, if you take my meaning, sir.

LUKE: Have you been in many battles?

THREEPIO: Several, I think. Actually, there's not much to tell. I'm not much more than an interpreter, and not very good at telling stories. Well, not at making them interesting, anyway.

Luke struggles to remove a small metal fragment from Artoo's neck joint. He uses a larger pick.

LUKE: Well, my little friend, you've got something jammed in here real good. Were you on a starcruiser or...

The fragment breaks loose with a snap, sending Luke tumbling head over heels. He sits up and sees a twelve-inch three-dimensional hologram of Leia Organa, the Rebel senator, being projected from the face of little Artoo. The image is a rainbow of colors as it flickers and

jiggles in the dimly lit garage. Luke's mouth hangs open in awe.

LEIA: Help me, Obi-Wan Kenobi. You're my only hope.

LUKE: What's this?

Artoo looks around and sheepishly beeps an answer for Threepio to translate. Leia continues to repeat the sentence fragment over and over.

THREEPIO: What is what?!? He asked you a question . . . (pointing at Leia) What is that?

Artoo whistles his surprise as he pretends to just notice the hologram. He looks around and sheepishly beeps an answer for Threepio to translate. Leia continues to repeat the sentence fragment over and over.

LEIA: Help me, Obi-Wan Kenobi. You're my only hope. Help me, Obi-Wan Kenobi. You're my only hope.

THREEPIO: Oh, he says it's nothing, sir. Merely a malfunction. Old data. Pay it no mind.

Luke becomes intrigued by the beautiful young girl.

LUKE: Who is she? She's beautiful.

THREEPIO: I'm afraid I'm not quite sure, sir.

LEIA: Help me, Obi-Wan Kenobi . . .

THREEPIO: I think she was a passenger on our last voyage. A person of some importance, sir—I believe. Our captain was attached to . . .

LUKE: Is there more to this recording?

Luke reaches for Artoo but he lets out several frantic squeaks and a whistle.

THREEPIO: Behave yourself, Artoo. You're going to get us in trouble. It's all right, you can trust him. He's our new master.

Artoo whistles and beeps a long message to Threepio.

THREEPIO: He says he's the property of Obi-Wan Kenobi, a resident of these parts. And it's a private message for him. Quite frankly, sir, I don't know what he's talking about. Our last master was Captain Antilles, but with what we've been through, this little R2 unit has become a bit eccentric.

LUKE: Obi-Wan Kenobi? I wonder if he means old Ben Kenobi?

THREEPIO: I beg your pardon, sir, but do you know what he's talking about?

LUKE: Well, I don't know anyone named Obi-Wan, but old Ben lives out beyond the dune sea. He's kind of a strange old hermit.

Luke gazes at the beautiful young princess for a few moments.

LUKE: I wonder who she is. It sounds like she's in trouble. I'd better play back the whole thing.

Artoo beeps something to Threepio.

THREEPIO: He says the restraining bolt has short circuited his recording system. He suggests that if you remove the bolt, he might be able to play back the entire recording.

Luke looks longingly at the lovely, little princess and hasn't really heard what Threepio has been saying.

LUKE: H'm? Oh, yeah, well, I guess you're too small to run away on me if I take this off! Okay.

Luke takes a wedged bar and pops the restraining bolt off Artoo's side.

LUKE: There you go.

The princess immediately disappears . . .

LUKE: Well, wait a minute. Where'd she go? Bring her back! Play back the entire message.

Above: Photograph of family Landspeeder, John Jay

Below: Sketch of Skyhopper, Joe Johnston

1 MILLENIUM FALCON GUNPORT TARGETING DEVICE

VIEW THIS SIDE

↑ UP

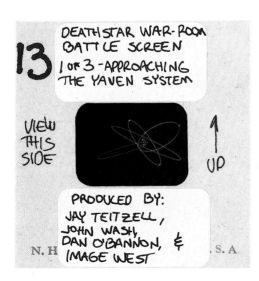

PRODUCED BY JAY TEITZELL

N. Hol   S. A.

2 TIE·FIGHTER IMPERIAL TARGETING DEVICE 1 OF 2

VIEW THIS SIDE

↑ UP

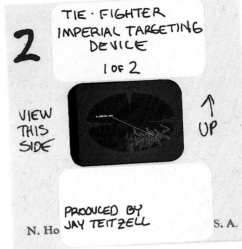

PRODUCED BY JAY TEITZELL

N. Ho   S. A.

3 SAME AS SLIDE #2 -LOCKED-ON TARGET- 2 OF 2

VIEW THIS SIDE

↑ UP

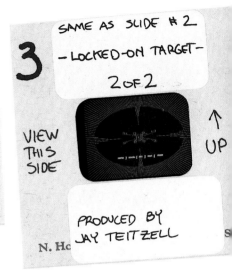

PRODUCED BY JAY TEITZELL

N. Ho   S.

7 SAME AS SLIDE #5,6 -SIGNAL TO FIRE- 3 OF 3

VIEW THIS SIDE

↑ UP

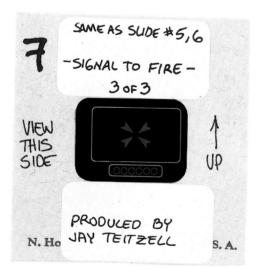

PRODUCED BY JAY TEITZELL

N. Ho   S. A.

8 LUKE'S LANDSPEEDER RADAR DEVICE -NOT USED IN FILM-

VIEW THIS SIDE

↑ UP

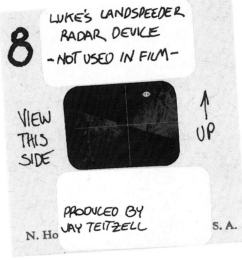

PRODUCED BY JAY TEITZELL

N. Ho   S. A.

9 FINAL DISPLAY OF STOLEN DATATAPES CONTENTS 1 OF 2 -SIMULATION OF SHIP DROPPING PHOTO TORPEDO AT DESIRED POINT

VIEW THIS SIDE

↑ UP

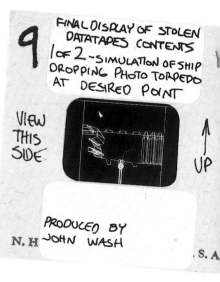

PRODUCED BY JOHN WASH

N. H   S. A

13 DEATH STAR WAR-ROOM BATTLE SCREEN 1 OF 3 -APPROACHING THE YAVEN SYSTEM

VIEW THIS SIDE

↑ UP

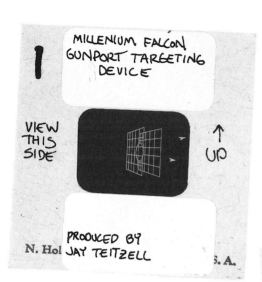

PRODUCED BY: JAY TEITZELL, JOHN WASH, DAN O'BANNON, & IMAGE WEST

N. H   S. A.

14 SEE SLIDE #13 2 OF 3 -APPROACH TO THE REBEL BASE (4TH MOON) COMING AROUND THE PLANET YAVEN

VIEW THIS SIDE

↑ UP

PRODUCED BY: JAY TEITZELL, JOHN WASH, DAN O'BANNON, & IMAGE WEST

N. H   S. A.

15 SEE SLIDES #13,14 3 OF 3 IN DIRECT LINE OF FIRE WITH THE FOURTH MOON OF YAVEN.

VIEW THIS SIDE

↑ UP

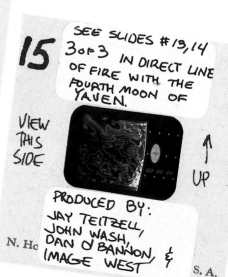

PRODUCED BY: JAY TEITZELL, JOHN WASH, DAN O'BANNON, & IMAGE WEST

N. Ho   S. A.

4 X & Y WING FIGHTER REBEL TARGETING DEVICE

VIEW THIS SIDE

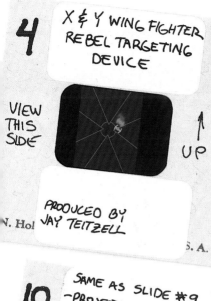

↑ UP

PRODUCED BY JAY TEITZELL

N. Ho   S. A.

5 X & Y WING FIGHTER PHOTON TORPEDO TARGETING COMPUTER 1 OF 3

VIEW THIS SIDE

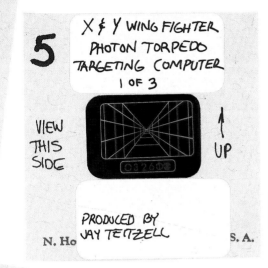

↑ UP

PRODUCED BY JAY TEITZELL

N. Ho   S. A.

6 SAME AS SLIDE # 5 —TARGET APPROACHING— 2 OF 3

VIEW THIS SIDE

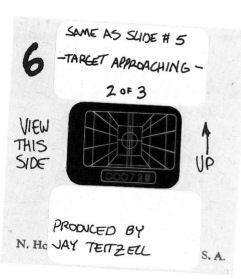

↑ UP

PRODUCED BY JAY TEITZELL

N. Ho   S. A.

10 SAME AS SLIDE #9 —PROJECTED RESULT OF DIRECT HIT TO DEATHSTAR THERMAL SHAFT 2 OF 2

VIEW THIS SIDE

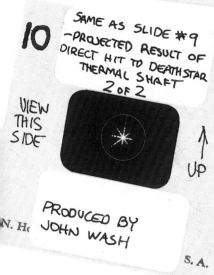

↑ UP

PRODUCED BY JOHN WASH

N. Ho   S. A.

11 FLOOR SCREEN DISPLAY AT REBEL BASE 1 OF 2 —SHOWS APPROACH OF DEATHSTAR

VIEW THIS SIDE

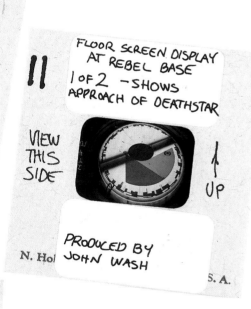

↑ UP

PRODUCED BY JOHN WASH

N. Ho   S. A.

12 SAME AS SLIDE # 11 2 OF 2 — DEATHSTAR NEARS POSITION FOR FIRING

VIEW THIS SIDE

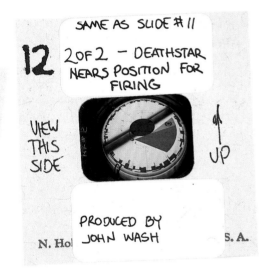

↑ UP

PRODUCED BY JOHN WASH

N. Ho   S. A.

16 DISPLAY SHOWS SEARCH FOR TRACTOR BEAM POWER SUPPLY

VIEW THIS SIDE

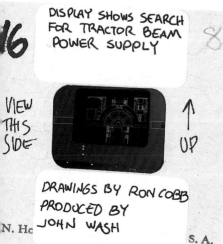

↑ UP

DRAWINGS BY RON COBB PRODUCED BY JOHN WASH

N. Ho   S. A.

17 MATTÉ ELEMENT FOR LUKE'S ELECTRO BINOCULARS 1 OF 2

VIEW THIS SIDE

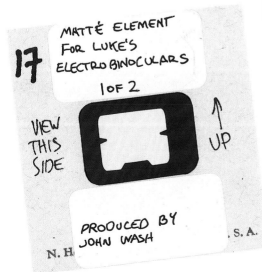

↑ UP

PRODUCED BY JOHN WASH

N. Ho   S. A.

18 DATA READOUT ELEMENTS USED WITH SLIDE # 17 2 OF 2

VIEW THIS SIDE

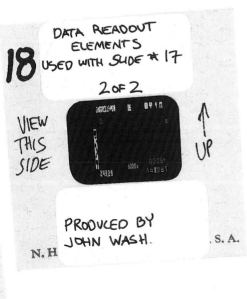

↑ UP

PRODUCED BY JOHN WASH.

N. Ho   S. A.

Computer Animation Graphics

Above: Sketch of Ben Kenobi,
John Mollo

Right: Sketches of Luke and Ben,
John Mollo

Artoo beeps an innocent reply as Threepio sits up in embarrassment.

THREEPIO: What message? The one you've just been playing. The one you're carrying inside your rusty innards!

A woman's voice calls out from the other room.

AUNT BERU: Luke? Luke! Come to dinner!

Luke stands up and shakes his head at the malfunctioning robot.

LUKE: All right, I'll be right there, Aunt Beru.

THREEPIO: I'm sorry, sir, but he appears to have picked up a slight flutter.

Luke tosses Artoo's restraining bolt on the workbench and hurries out of the room.

LUKE: Well, see what you can do with him. I'll be right back.

THREEPIO: (to Artoo) Just you reconsider playing that message for him.

Artoo beeps in response.

THREEPIO: No, I don't think he likes you at all.

Artoo beeps.

THREEPIO: No, I don't like you either.

INTERIOR: LAR'S HOMESTEAD–DINING AREA

Luke's Aunt Beru, a warm, motherly woman, fills a pitcher with blue fluid from a refrigerated container in the well-used kitchen. She puts the pitcher on a tray with some bowls of food and starts for the dining area.

Luke sits with his Uncle Owen before a table covered with steaming bowls of food as Aunt Beru carries in a bowl of red grain.

LUKE: You know, I think that R2 unit we bought might have been stolen.

OWEN: What makes you think that?

LUKE: Well, I stumbled across a recording while I was cleaning him. He says he belongs to someone called Obi-Wan Kenobi.

Owen is greatly alarmed at the mention of this name, but manages to control himself.

LUKE: I thought he might have meant old Ben. Do you know what he's talking about? Well, I wonder if he's related to Ben.

Owen breaks loose with a fit of uncontrolled anger.

OWEN: That old man's just a crazy wizard. Tomorrow I want you to take that R2 unit into Anchorhead and have its memory flushed. That'll be the end of it. It belongs to us now.

LUKE: But what if this Obi-Wan comes looking for him?

OWEN: He won't. I don't think he exists any more. He died about the same time as your father.

LUKE: He knew my father?

OWEN: I told you to forget it. Your only concern is to prepare the new droids for tomorrow. In the morning I want them on the south ridge working on those condensers.

LUKE: Yes, sir. I think those new droids are going to work out fine. In fact, I, uh, was also thinking about our agreement about my staying on another season. And if these new droids do work out, I want to transmit my application to the Academy this year.

Owen's face becomes a scowl, although he tries to suppress it.

OWEN: You mean the next semester before harvest?

LUKE: Sure, there're more than enough droids.

OWEN: Harvest is when I need you the most. Only one more season. This year we'll make enough on the harvest so I'll be able to hire some more hands. And then you can go to the Academy next year.

Luke continues to toy with his food, not looking at his uncle.

OWEN: You must understand I need you here, Luke.

LUKE: But it's a whole 'nother year.

OWEN: Look, it's only one more season.

Luke pushes his half-eaten plate of food aside and stands.

LUKE: Yeah, that's what you said last year when Biggs and Tank left.

AUNT BERU: Where are you going?

LUKE: It looks like I'm going nowhere. I have to finish cleaning those droids.

Resigned to his fate, Luke paddles out of the room. Owen mechanically finishes his dinner.

AUNT BERU: Owen, he can't stay here forever. Most of his friends have gone. It means so much to him.

OWEN: I'll make it up to him next year. I promise.

AUNT BERU: Luke's just not a farmer, Owen. He has too much of his father in him.

OWEN: That's what I'm afraid of.

EXTERIOR: TATOOINE—LARS HOMESTEAD

The giant twin suns of Tatooine slowly disappear behind a distant dune range. Luke stands watching them for a few

moments, then reluctantly enters the domed entrance to the homestead.

INTERIOR: LARS HOMESTEAD—GARAGE

Luke enters the garage to discover the robots nowhere in sight. He takes a small control box from his utility belt similar to the one the Jawas were carrying. He activates the box, which creates a low hum, and Threepio, letting out a short yell, pops up from behind the Skyhopper spaceship.

LUKE: What are you doing hiding there?

Threepio stumbles forward, but Artoo is still nowhere in sight.

THREEPIO: It wasn't my fault, sir. Please don't deactivate me. I told him not to go, but he's faulty, malfunctioning; kept babbling on about his mission.

LUKE: Oh, no!

Luke races out of the garage followed by Threepio.

EXTERIOR: TATOOINE—LARS HOMESTEAD

Luke rushes out of the small domed entry to the homestead and searches the darkening horizon for the small triped astro-robot. Threepio struggles out of the homestead and on the salt flat as Luke scans the landscape with his electrobinoculars.

THREEPIO: That R2 unit has always been a problem. These astro-droids are getting quite out of hand. Even I can't understand their logic at times.

LUKE: How could I be so stupid? He's nowhere in sight. Blast it!

THREEPIO: Pardon me, sir, but couldn't we go after him?

LUKE: It's too dangerous with all the Sandpeople around. We'll have to wait until morning.

Owen yells up from the homestead plaza.

OWEN: Luke, I'm shutting the power down for the night.

LUKE: All right, I'll be there in a few minutes. Boy, am I gonna get it.

He takes one final look across the dim horizon.

You know that little droid is going to cause me a lot of trouble.

THREEPIO: Oh, he excels at that, sir.

INTERIOR: LARS HOMESTEAD—PLAZA

Morning slowly creeps into the sparse but sparkling oasis of the open courtyard. The idyll is broken by the yelling of Uncle Owen, his voice echoing throughout the homestead.

OWEN: Luke? Luke? Luke? Where could he be loafing now!

INTERIOR: LARS HOMESTEAD—KITCHEN

The interior of the kitchen is a warm glow as Aunt Beru prepares the morning breakfast. Owen enters in a huff.

OWEN: Have you seen Luke this morning?

AUNT BERU: He said he had some things to do before he started today, so he left early.

OWEN: Uh? Did he take those two new droids with him?

AUNT BERU: I think so.

OWEN: Well, he'd better have those units in the south range repaired by midday or there'll be hell to pay!

Right: Photograph of Aunt Beru's
kitchen set, John Jay

Below: Drawing of kitchen set,
John Barry

Above: Sketch, John Barry

Above: Thumbnail sketch and production painting, Ralph McQuarrie

EXTERIOR: TATOOINE—DESERT WASTELAND—LUKE'S SPEEDER—DAY

The rock and sand of the desert floor are a blur as Threepio pilots the sleek Landspeeder gracefully across the vast wasteland.

INTERIOR/EXTERIOR: LUKE'S SPEEDER—DESERT WASTELAND—TRAVELING—DAY

Luke leans over the back of the speeder and adjusts something in the motor compartment.

LUKE: (yelling) How's that.

Threepio signals that it is fine and Luke turns back into the wind-whipped cockpit and pops the canopy shut.

LUKE: Old Ben Kenobi lives out in this direction somewhere, but I don't see how that R2 unit could have come this far. We must have missed him. Uncle

Owen isn't going to take this very well.

THREEPIO: Sir, would it help if you told him it was my fault.

LUKE: (brightening) Sure. He needs you. He'd probably only deactivate you for a day or so...

THREEPIO: Deactivate! Well, on the other hand if you hadn't removed his restraining bolt...

LUKE: Wait, there's something dead ahead on the scanner. It looks like our droid...hit the accelerator.

EXTERIOR: TATOOINE—ROCK MESA—DUNE SEA—COASTLINE—DAY

From high on a rock mesa, the tiny Landspeeder can be seen gliding across the desert floor. Suddenly in the foreground two weather-beaten Sandpeople shrouded in their grimy desert cloaks peer over the edge of the rock mesa. One of the marginally human creatures raises a long ominous laser rifle and points it at the speeder but the second creature grabs the gun before it can be fired.

The Sandpeople, or Tusken Raiders as they're sometimes called, speak in a coarse barbaric languages as they get into an animated argument. The second Tusken Raider seems to get in the final word and the nomads scurry over the rocky terrain.

EXTERIOR: TATOOINE—ROCK MESA—CANYON

The Tusken Raiders approach two large Banthas standing tied to a rock. The monstrous, bear-like creatures are as large as elephants, with huge red eyes, tremendous looped horns, and long, furry, dinosaur-like tails. The Tusken Raiders mount saddles strapped to the huge creatures' shaggy backs and ride off down the rugged bluff.

EXTERIOR: TATOOINE—ROCK CANYON—FLOOR

The speeder is parked on the floor of a massive canyon. Luke, with his long laser rifle slung over his shoulder, stands before little Artoo.

LUKE: Hey, whoa, just where do you think you're going?

The little droid whistles a feeble reply, as Threepio poses menacingly behind the little runaway.

THREEPIO: Master Luke here is your rightful owner. We'll have no more of this Obi-Wan Kenobi jibberish...and don't talk to me of your mission, either. You're fortunate he doesn't blast you into a million pieces right here.

LUKE: Well, come on. It's getting late. I only hope we can get back before Uncle Owen really blows up.

THREEPIO: If you don't mind my saying so, sir, I think you should deactivate the little fugitive until you've gotten him back to your workshop.

LUKE: No, he's not going to try anything.

Suddenly the little robot jumps to life with a mass of frantic whistles and screams.

LUKE: What's wrong with him now?

THREEPIO: Oh my...sir, he says there are several creatures approaching from the southeast.

Luke swings his rifle into position and looks to the south.

LUKE: Sandpeople! Or worse! Come on, let's go have a look. Come on.

EXTERIOR: TATOOINE—ROCK CANYON—RIDGE—DAY

Luke carefully makes his way to the top of a rock ridge and scans the canyon with his electrobinoculars. He spots the

two riderless Banthas. Threepio struggles up behind the young adventurer.

LUKE: There are two Banthas down there but I don't see any...wait a second, they're Sandpeople all right. I can see one of them now.

Luke watches the distant Tusken Raider through his electrobinoculars. Suddenly something huge moves in front of his field of view. Before Luke or Threepio can react, a large, gruesome Tusken Raider looms over them. Threepio is startled and backs away, right off the side of the cliff. He can be heard for several moments as he clangs, bangs and rattles down the side of the mountain.

The towering creature brings down his curved, double-pointed gaderffii—the dreaded axe blade that has struck terror in the heart of the local settlers. But Luke

manages to block the blow with his laser rifle, which is smashed to pieces. The terrified farm boy scrambles backward until he is forced to the edge of a deep crevice. The sinister Raider stands over him with his weapon raised and lets out a horrible shrieking laugh.

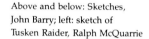

Above and below: Sketches, John Barry; left: sketch of Tusken Raider, Ralph McQuarrie

EXTERIOR: TATOOINE—ROCK CANYON—FLOOR—DAY

Artoo forces himself into the shadows of a small alcove in the rocks as the vicious Sandpeople walk past carrying the inert Luke Skywalker, who is dropped in a heap before the speeder. The Sandpeople ransack the speeder, throwing parts and supplies in all directions. Suddenly they stop. Then everything is quiet for a few moments. A great howling moan is heard echoing throughout the canyon which sends the Sandpeople fleeing in terror.

Artoo moves even tighter into the shadows as the slight swishing sound that frightened off the Sandpeople grows even closer, until a shabby old desert-rat-of-a-man appears and leans over Luke. His ancient leathery face, cracked and weathered by exotic climates is set off by dark, penetrating eyes and a scraggly white beard. Ben Kenobi squints his eyes as he scrutinizes the unconscious farm boy. Artoo makes a slight sound and Ben turns and looks right at him.

BEN: Hello there! Come here, my little friend. Don't be afraid.

Artoo waddles over to where Luke lies crumpled in a heap and begins to whistle and beep his concern. Ben puts his hand on Luke's forehead and he begins to come around.

BEN: Don't worry, he'll be all right.

LUKE: What happened?

BEN: Rest easy, son, you've had a busy day. You're fortunate you're still in one piece.

LUKE: Ben? Ben Kenobi! Boy, am I glad to see you!

BEN: The Jundland wastes are not to be traveled lightly. Tell me, young Luke, what brings you out this far?

LUKE: Oh, this little droid! I think he's searching for his former master...I've never seen such devotion in a droid before...there seems to be no stopping him. He claims to be the property of an Obi-Wan Kenobi. Is he a relative of yours? Do you know who he's talking about?

Ben ponders this for a moment, scratching his scruffy beard.

BEN: Obi-Wan Kenobi...Obi-Wan? Now that's a name I haven't heard in a long time...a long time.

LUKE: I think my uncle knew him. He said he was dead...

BEN: Oh, he's not dead, not...not yet.

LUKE: You know him!

BEN: Well of course, of course I know him. He's me! I haven't gone by the name Obi-Wan since oh, before you were born.

LUKE: Then this droid does belong to you.

BEN: Don't seem to remember ever owning a droid. Very interesting...

He suddenly looks up at the overhanging cliffs.

BEN: I think we better get indoors. The Sandpeople are easily startled but they will soon be back and in greater numbers.

Luke sits up and rubs his head. Artoo lets out a pathetic beep causing Luke to remember something. He looks around.

LUKE: ...Threepio!

EXTERIOR: TATOOINE—SAND PIT—ROCK MESA—DAY

Little Artoo stands at the edge of a large sand pit and begins to chatter away in electronic whistles and beeps. Luke and Ben stand over a very dented and tangled Threepio lying half buried in the sand. One of his arms has broken off.

Right: Photograph of Ben Kenobi's dwelling; below: early sketch of Luke, Ralph McQuarrie

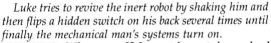

Luke tries to revive the inert robot by shaking him and then flips a hidden switch on his back several times until finally the mechanical man's systems turn on.

THREEPIO: Where am I? I must have taken a bad step...

LUKE: Can you stand? We've got to get out of here before the Sandpeople return.

THREEPIO: I don't think I can make it. You go on, Master Luke. There's no sense in you risking yourself on my account. I'm done for.

Artoo makes a beeping sound.

LUKE: No, you're not. What kind of talk is that?

Luke and Ben help the battered robot to his feet. Little Artoo watches from the top of the pit. Ben glances around suspiciously. Sensing something, he stands up and sniffs the air.

BEN: Quickly, son...they're on the move.

INTERIOR: KENOBI'S DWELLING

The small, spartan hovel is cluttered with desert junk but still manages to radiate an air of time-worn comfort and security. Luke is in one corner repairing Threepio's arm, as old Ben sits thinking.

LUKE: No, my father didn't fight in the wars. He was a navigator on a spice freighter.

BEN: That's what your uncle told you. He didn't

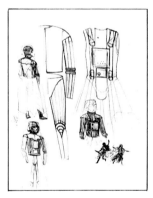

Above: Sketches of Darth Vader, John Mollo

BEN: Your father's lightsaber. This is the weapon of a Jedi Knight. Not as clumsy or as random as a blaster.

Luke pushes a button on the handle. A long beam shoots out about four feet and flickers there. The light plays across the ceiling.

BEN: An elegant weapon for a more civilized time. For over a thousand generations the Jedi Knights were the guardians of peace and justice in the Old Republic. Before the dark times, before the Empire.

Luke hasn't really been listening.

LUKE: How did my father die?

BEN: A young Jedi named Darth Vader, who was a pupil of mine until he turned to evil, helped the Empire hunt down and destroy the Jedi Knights. He betrayed and murdered your father. Now the Jedi are all but extinct. Vader was seduced by the dark side of the Force.

LUKE: The Force?

BEN: Well, the Force is what gives the Jedi his power. It's an energy field created by all living things. It surrounds us and penetrates us. It binds the galaxy together.

Artoo makes beeping sounds.

BEN: Now, let's see if we can't figure out what you are, my little friend. And where you come from.

LUKE: I saw part of the message he was....

Luke is cut short as the recorded image of the beautiful young Rebel princess is projected from Artoo's face.

BEN: I seem to have found it.

Luke stops his work as the lovely girl's image flickers before his eyes.

LEIA: General Kenobi, years ago you served my father in the Clone Wars. Now he begs you to help him in his struggle against the Empire. I regret that I am unable to present my father's request to you in person, but my ship has fallen under attack and I'm afraid my mission to bring you to Alderaan has failed. I have placed information vital to the survival of the Rebellion into the memory systems of this R2 unit. My father will know how to retrieve it. You must see this droid safely delivered to him on Alderaan. This is our most desperate hour. Help me, Obi-Wan Kenobi, you're my only hope.

There is a little static and the transmission is cut short. Old Ben leans back and scratches his head. He silently puffs on a tarnished chrome water pipe. Luke has stars in his eyes.

BEN: You must learn the ways of the Force if you're to come with me to Alderaan.

LUKE: (laughing) Alderaan? I'm not going to Alderaan? I've got to go home. It's late, I'm in for it as it is.

BEN: I need your help, Luke. She needs your help. I'm getting too old for this sort of thing.

LUKE: I can't get involved! I've got work to do! It's not that I like the Empire. I hate it! But there's nothing I can do about it right now. It's such a long way from here.

BEN: That's your uncle talking.

LUKE: (sighing) Oh, God, my uncle. How am I ever going to explain this?

BEN: Learn about the Force, Luke.

LUKE: Look, I can take you as far as Anchorhead. You can get a transport there to Mos Eisley or wherever you're going.

BEN: You must do what you feel is right, of course.

hold with your father's ideals. Thought he should have stayed here and not gotten involved.

LUKE: You fought in the Clone Wars?

BEN: Yes, I was once a Jedi Knight the same as your father.

LUKE: I wish I'd known him.

BEN: He was the best star-pilot in the galaxy, and a cunning warrior. I understand you've become quite a good pilot yourself. And he was a good friend. Which reminds me...

Ben gets up and goes to a chest where he rummages around. As Luke finishes repairing Threepio and starts to fit the restraining bolt back on, Threepio looks at him nervously. Luke thinks about the bolt for a moment then puts it on the table. Ben shuffles up and presents Luke with a short handle with several electronic gadgets attached to it.

BEN: I have something here for you. Your father wanted you to have this when you were old enough, but your uncle wouldn't allow it. He feared you might follow old Obi-Wan on some damned-fool idealistic crusade like your father did.

THREEPIO: Sir, if you'll not be needing me, I'll close down for a while.

LUKE: Sure, go ahead.

Ben hands Luke the saber.

LUKE: What is it?

Ben Kenobi Costume Sketches

Right: John Mollo; below:
Ralph McQuarrie;
opposite page: John Mollo

EXTERIOR: SPACE

An Imperial Stardestroyer heads toward the evil planet-like battle station: the Death Star!

INTERIOR: DEATH STAR—CONFERENCE ROOM

Eight Imperial senators and generals sit around a black conference table. Imperial stormtroopers stand guard around the room. Commander Tagge, a young, slimy-looking general, is speaking.

TAGGE: Until this battle station is fully operational we are vulnerable. The Rebel Alliance is too well equipped. They're more dangerous than you realize.

The bitter Admiral Motti twists nervously in his chair.

MOTTI: Dangerous to your starfleet, Commander; not to this battle station!

TAGGE: The Rebellion will continue to gain a support in the Imperial Senate as long as. . . .

Suddenly all heads turn as Commander Tagge's speech is cut short and the Grand Moff Tarkin, governor of the Imperial outland regions, enters. He is followed by his powerful ally, The Sith Lord, Darth Vader. All of the generals stand and bow before the thin, evil-looking governor as he takes his place at the head of the table. The Dark Lord stands behind him.

TARKIN: The Imperial Senate will no longer be of any concern to us. I've just received word that the Emperor has dissolved the council permanently. The last remnants of the Old Republic have been swept away.

TAGGE: That's impossible! How will the Emperor maintain control without the bureaucracy?

TARKIN: The regional governors now have direct control over territories. Fear will keep the local systems in line. Fear of this battle station.

TAGGE: And what of the Rebellion? If the Rebels have obtained a complete technical readout of this station, it is possible, however unlikely, that they might find a weakness and exploit it.

VADER: The plans you refer to will soon be back in our hands.

MOTTI: Any attack made by the Rebels against this station would be a useless gesture, no matter what technical data they've obtained. This station is now the ultimate power in the universe. I suggest we use it!

VADER: Don't be too proud of this technological terror you've constructed. The ability to destroy a planet is insignificant next to the power of the Force.

MOTTI: Don't try to frighten us with your sorcerer's ways, Lord Vader. Your sad devotion to that ancient religion has not helped you conjure up the stolen data tapes, or given you clairvoyance enough to find the Rebel's hidden fort. . .

Suddenly Motti chokes and starts to turn blue under Vader's spell.

VADER: I find your lack of faith disturbing.

TARKIN: Enough of this! Vader, release him!

VADER: As you wish.

TARKIN: This bickering is pointless. Lord Vader will provide us with the location of the Rebel fortress by the time this station is operational. We will then crush the Rebellion with one swift stroke.

EXTERIOR: TATOOINE—WASTELAND

The speeder stops before what remains of the huge Jawa Sandcrawler. Luke and Ben walk among the smoldering rubble and scattered bodies.

LUKE: It looks like Sandpeople did this, all right. Look, here are Gaffi sticks, Bantha tracks. It's just. . . I never heard of them hitting anything this big before.

Ben is crouching in the sand studying the tracks.

BEN: They didn't. But we are meant to think they did. These tracks are side by side. Sandpeople always ride single file to hide their numbers.

LUKE: These are the same Jawas that sold us Artoo and Threepio.

BEN: And these blast points, too accurate for Sandpeople. Only Imperial stormtroopers are so precise.

Below: Sketch of Darth Vader, Ralph McQuarrie

LUKE: Why would Imperial troops want to slaughter Jawas?

Luke looks back at the speeder where Artoo and Threepio are inspecting the dead Jawas, and puts two and two together.

LUKE: If they traced the robots here, they may have learned who they sold them to. And that would lead them back home!

Luke reaches a sudden horrible realization, then races for the speeder and jumps in.

BEN: Wait, Luke! It's too dangerous.

Luke races off leaving Ben and the two robots alone with the burning Sandcrawler.

EXTERIOR: TATOOINE—WASTELAND

Luke races across the flat landscape in his battered Landspeeder.

EXTERIOR: TATOOINE—LARS HOMESTEAD

The speeder roars up to the burning homestead. Luke jumps out and runs to the smoking holes that were once his home. Debris is scattered everywhere and it looks as if a great battle has taken place.

LUKE: Uncle Owen! Aunt Beru! Uncle Owen!

Luke stumbles around in a daze looking for his aunt and uncle. Suddenly he comes upon their smoldering remains. He is stunned, and cannot speak. Hate replaces fear and a new resolve comes over him.

EXTERIOR: SPACE

Imperial TIE fighters race toward the Death Star.

INTERIOR: DEATH STAR—DETENTION CORRIDOR

Two stormtroopers open an electronic cell door and allow several Imperial guards to enter. Princess Leia's face is filled with defiance, which slowly gives way to fear as a giant black torture robot enters, followed by Darth Vader.

VADER: And now, Your Highness, we will discuss the location of your hidden Rebel base.

The torture robot gives off a steady beeping sound as it approaches Princess Leia and extends one of its mechanical arms bearing a large hypodermic needle. The door slides shut and the long cell block hallway appears peaceful. The muffled screams of the Rebel princess are barely heard.

EXTERIOR: TATOOINE—WASTELAND

There is a large bonfire of Jawa bodies blazing in front of the Sandcrawler as Ben and the robots finish burning the dead. Luke drives up in the speeder and Ben walks over to him.

BEN: There's nothing you could have done, Luke, had you been there. You'd have been killed, too, and the droids would now be in the hands of the Empire.

LUKE: I want to come with you to Alderaan. There's nothing here for me now. I want to learn the ways of the Force and become a Jedi like my father.

EXTERIOR: TATOOINE—WASTELAND

The Landspeeder with Luke, Artoo, Threepio, and Ben in it zooms across the desert. The speeder stops on a bluff overlooking the spaceport at Mos Eisley. It is a haphazard array of low, grey, concrete structures and semi-domes. A harsh gale blows across the stark canyon floor. Luke adjusts his goggles and walks to the edge of the craggy bluff where Ben is standing.

BEN: Mos Eisley Spaceport. You will never find a more wretched hive of scum and villainy. We must be cautious.

Ben looks over at Luke, who gives the old Jedi a determined smile.

EXTERIOR: TATOOINE—MOS EISLEY—STREET

The speeder is stopped on a crowded street by several combat-hardened stormtroopers who look over the two robots. A Trooper questions Luke.

TROOPER: How long have you had these droids?

LUKE: About three or four seasons.

BEN: They're for sale if you want them.

Below: Drawing of torture robot, Ralph McQuarrie

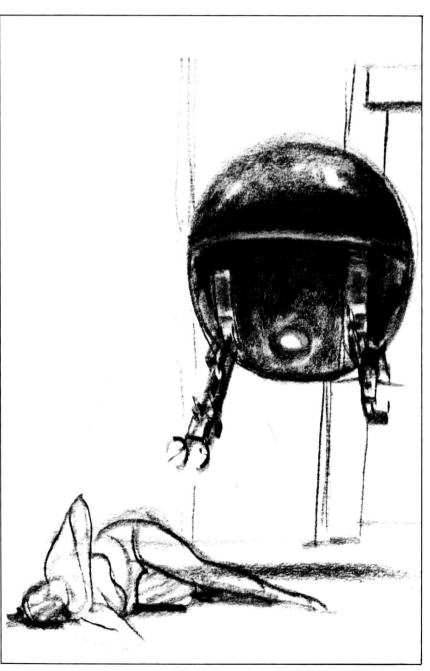

Right: Costume sketch of Imperial
officers, John Mollo

Sketch of Imperial guard,
Ralph McQuarrie

Sketches of Imperial officers,
guards, and pilots, Johr Mollo

TROOPER: Let me see your identification.

Luke becomes very nervous as he fumbles to find his ID while Ben speaks to the Trooper in a very controlled voice.

BEN: You don't need to see his identification.

TROOPER: We don't need to see his identification.

BEN: These are not the droids you're looking for.

TROOPER: These are not the droids we're looking for.

BEN: He can go about his business.

TROOPER: You can go about your business.

BEN: (to Luke) Move along.

TROOPER: Move along. Move along.

EXTERIOR: TATOOINE—MOS EISLEY—STREET

The speeder pulls up in front of a rundown blockhouse cantina on the outskirts of the spaceport. Various strange forms of transport, including several unusual beasts of burden, are parked outside the bar. A Jawa runs up and begins to fondle the speeder.

THREEPIO: I can't abide these Jawas. Disgusting creatures.

As Luke gets out of the speeder he tries to shoo the Jawa away.

LUKE: Go on, go on. I can't understand how we got by those troopers. I thought we were dead.

BEN: The Force can have a strong influence on the weak-minded. You will find it a powerful ally.

LUKE: Do you really think we're going to find a pilot here that'll take us to Alderaan?

BEN: Well, most of the best freighter pilots can be found here. Only watch your step. This place can be a little rough.

LUKE: I'm ready for anything.

THREEPIO: Come along, Artoo.

INTERIOR: TATOOINE—MOS EISLEY—CANTINA

The young adventurer and his two mechanical servants follow Ben Kenobi into the smoke-filled cantina. The murky, moldy den is filled with a startling array of weird and exotic alien creatures and monsters at the long metallic bar. At first the sight is horrifying. One-eyed, thousand-eyed, slimy, furry, scaly, tentacled, and clawed

creatures huddle over drinks. Ben moves to an empty spot at the bar near a group of repulsive but human scum. A huge, rough-looking Bartender stops Luke and the robots.

BARTENDER: We don't serve their kind here!

Luke still recovering from the shock of seeing so many outlandish creatures, doesn't quite catch the bartender's drift.

LUKE: What?

BARTENDER: Your droids. They'll have to wait outside. We don't want them here.

Luke looks to old Ben, who is busy talking to one of the Galactic pirates. He notices that several of the gruesome creatures along the bar are giving him a very unfriendly glare.

Luke pats Threepio on the shoulder.

LUKE: Listen, why don't you wait out by the speeder. We don't want any trouble.

THREEPIO: I heartily agree with you sir.

Threepio and his stubby partner go outside and most of the creatures at the bar go back to their drinks.

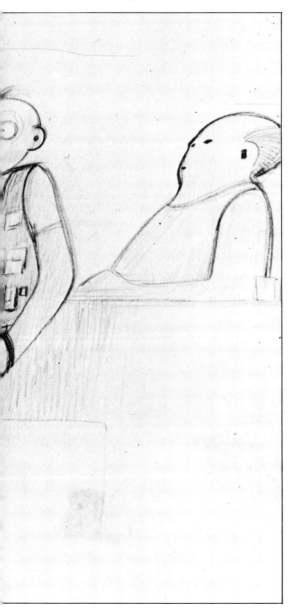

Ben is standing next to Chewbacca, an eight-foot-tall-savage-looking creature resembling a huge grey bushbaby monkey with fierce baboon-like fangs. His large blue eyes dominate a fur-covered face and soften his otherwise awesome appearance. Over his matted, furry body he wears two chrome bandoliers, and little else. He is a two-hundred-year-old Wookiee and a sight to behold.

Ben speaks to the Wookiee, pointing to Luke several times during his conversation and the huge creature suddenly lets out a horrifying laugh. Luke is more than a little bit disconcerted and pretends not to hear the conversation between Ben and the giant Wookiee.

Luke is terrified but tries not to show it. He quietly sips his drink, looking over the crowd for a more sympathetic ear or whatever.

A large, multiple-eyed Creature gives Luke a rough shove.

CREATURE: Negola dewaghi wooldugger?!?

The hideous freak is obviously drunk. Luke tries to ignore the creature and turns back on his drink. A short, grubby Human and an even smaller rodent-like beast join the belligerent monstrosity.

HUMAN: He doesn't like you.

LUKE: I'm sorry.

HUMAN: I don't like you either.

The big creature is getting agitated and yells some unintelligible gibberish at the now rather nervous, young adventurer.

HUMAN: (continued) Don't insult us. You just watch yourself. We're wanted men. I have the death sentence on twelve systems.

LUKE: I'll be careful then.

HUMAN: You'll be dead.

The rodent lets out a loud grunt and everything at the bar moves away. Luke tries to remain cool but it isn't easy. His three adversaries ready their weapons. Old Ben moves in behind Luke.

BEN: This little one isn't worth the effort. Come let me buy you something...

A powerful blow from the unpleasant creature sends the young would-be Jedi sailing across the room, crashing through tables and breaking a large jug filled with a foul-looking liquid. With a blood-curdling shriek, the monster draws a wicked chrome laser pistol from his belt and levels it at old Ben. The bartender panics.

BARTENDER: No blasters! No blasters!

With astounding agility old Ben's laser sword sparks to life and in a flash an arm lies on the floor. The rodent is cut in two and the giant multiple-eyed creature lies doubled, cut from chin to groin. Ben carefully and precisely turns off his laser sword and replaces it on his utility belt. Luke, shaking and totally amazed at the old man's abilities, attempts to stand. The entire fight has lasted only a matter of seconds. The cantina goes back to normal, although Ben is given a respectable amount of room at the bar. Luke, rubbing his bruised head, approaches the old man with new awe. Ben points to the Wookiee.

BEN: This is Chewbacca. He's first-mate on a ship that might suit our needs.

EXTERIOR: TATOOINE—MOS EISLEY—STREET

Threepio paces in front of the cantina as Artoo carries on an electronic conversation with another little red astro-droid. A creature comes out of the cantina and approaches two stormtroopers in the street.

THREEPIO: I don't like the look of this.

Left: Sketch of Cantina characters, John Mollo; below: drawing of Han Solo, John Mollo

Sketches of Cantina characters,
John Mollo

ocals (farmers)

⑥ 2 × FARMERS
FRED WOOD, ROY STAITE, ANTHONY LANG
ROBERT DAVIES , SALO GARDNER
JEFF MOON

⑦ 3 × CORELLIAN PIRATES
BARRY COPPING

⑧ 3 × STARPILOTS
DIANA SADLEY WAY
3 martian

martian hen
3 radiation
masks

SKETCH
colour.

Brown shirt.
Khaki.
Stone.

BERBERTA
DENHAM

④ 4 × LOCAL UGLI MEN
ERICA SIMMONS
ANNETTE JONES

⑤ 1 × GRASSHOPPER
TOMMY ILSLEY
JOE KAYE.

⑯ 3 × PLUTONIAN martian

BARRY GNOME

NOTE
㉔ ORCHESTRA : This consists of 4 m
1 × No3 ; 1 × No7 ; + 2 othe
㉕ Jawas Not shown
㉖ Stormtroopers Not shown

TURGEON

SKETCH.

SKETCH.

½ 6 midget

FLASH GORDON MIDGET
Marcus Powell
GILDA COHEN BERN
LITTLE-PRINT BERN

S KETCH.

4-3-76.

㉑ 2 × WALRUS

㉒ 1 × COLONEL

㉓ 1 × BAT

Sketches of Cantina creatures and production painting, Ralph McQuarrie; photograph of inside the entrance to the Cantina set, John Jay

Drawing of Cantina character. John Mollo

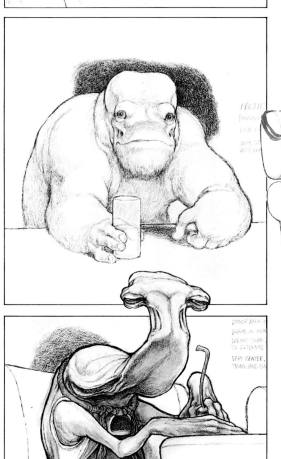

Cantina sketches, Ron Cobb

Cantina creature sketches,
Ralph McQuarrie

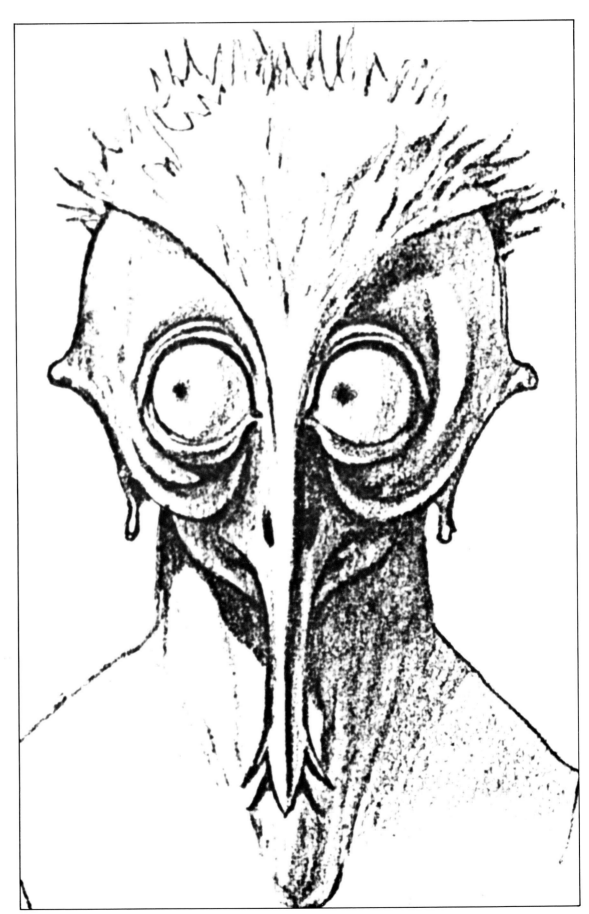

INTERIOR: TATOOINE—MOS EISLEY—CANTINA

Strange creatures play exotic big band music on odd-looking instruments as Luke, still giddy, downs a fresh drink and follows Ben and Chewbacca to a booth where Han Solo is sitting. Han is a tough, roguish starpilot about thirty years old. A mercenary on a starship, he is simple, sentimental, and cocksure.

HAN: Han Solo. I'm captain of the Millennium Falcon. Chewie here tells me you're looking for passage to the Alderaan system.

BEN: Yes, indeed. If it's a fast ship.

HAN: Fast ship? You've never heard of the Millennium Falcon?

BEN: Should I have?

HAN: It's the ship that made the Kessel run in less than twelve parsecs!

Ben reacts to Solo's stupid attempt to impress them with obvious misinformation.

HAN: (continued) I've outrun Imperial starships, not the local bulk-cruisers, mind you. I'm talking about the big Corellian ships now. She's fast enough for you, old man. What's the cargo?

BEN: Only passengers. Myself, the boy, two droids, and no questions asked.

HAN: What is it? Some kind of local trouble?

BEN: Let's just say we'd like to avoid any Imperial entanglements.

HAN: Well, that's the real trick, isn't it? And it's going to cost you something extra. Ten thousand in advance.

LUKE: Ten thousand? We could almost buy our own ship for that!

Right: Early sketch of Chewbacca,
Ralph McQuarrie; center: Han
and Chewbacca, John Mollo

Left and below. Sketches of
Chewbacca, Ralph McQuarrie

Han Solo
Facing page: Han and Luke,
Ralph McQuarrie

Left: John Mollo; center:
photograph, Bob Seidemann

Below: Ralph McQuarrie

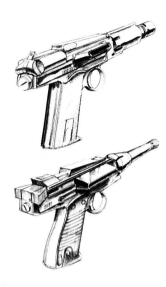

Sketches of guns,
Ralph McQuarrie

HAN: But who's going to fly it, kid! You?
LUKE: You bet I could. I'm not such a bad pilot myself! We don't have to sit here and listen...
BEN: We haven't that much with us. But we could pay you two thousand now, plus fifteen when we reach Alderaan.
HAN: Seventeen, huh!

Han ponders this for a few moments.

HAN: Okay. You guys got yourself a ship. We'll leave as soon as you're ready. Docking Bay Ninety-four.
BEN: Ninety-four.
HAN: Looks like somebody's beginning to take an interest in your handiwork.

Ben and Luke turn around to see four Imperial stormtroopers looking at the dead bodies and asking the bartenders some questions. The bartender points to the booth.

TROOPER: All right, we'll check it out.

The stormtroopers look over at the booth but Luke and Ben are gone. The bartender shrugs his shoulders in puzzlement.

HAN: Seventeen thousand! Those guys must really be desperate. This could really save my neck. Get back to the ship and get her ready.

EXTERIOR: TATOOINE—MOS EISLEY—STREET

BEN: You'll have to sell your speeder.
LUKE: That's okay. I'm never coming back to this planet again.

INTERIOR: MOS EISLEY—CANTINA

As Han is about leave, Greedo, slimy green-faced alien with a short trunk-nose, pokes a gun in his side. The creature speaks in a foreign tongue translated into English subtitles.

GREEDO: Going somewhere, Solo?
HAN: Yes, Greedo. As a matter of fact, I was just going to see your boss. Tell Jabba that I've got his money.

Han sits down and the alien sits across from him holding the gun on him.

GREEDO: It's too late. You should have paid him when you had the chance. Jabba's put a price on your head, so large that every bounty hunter in the galaxy will be looking for you. I'm lucky I found you first.
HAN: Yeah, but this time I got the money.
GREEDO: If you give it to me, I might forget I found you.
HAN: I don't have it with me. Tell Jabba...
GREEDO: Jabba's through with you. He has no time for smugglers who drop their shipments at the first sign of an Imperial cruiser.
HAN: Even I get boarded sometimes. Do you think I had a choice?

Han Solo slowly reaches for his gun under the table.

GREEDO: You can tell that to Jabba. He may only take your ship.
HAN: Over my dead body.
GREEDO: That's the idea. I've been looking forward to killing you for a long time.
HAN: Yes, I'll bet you have.

Suddenly the slimy alien disappears in a blinding flash of light. Han pulls his smoking gun from beneath the table as the other patrons look on in bemused amazement. Han gets up and starts out of the cantina, flipping the bartender some coins as he leaves.

HAN: Sorry about the mess.

EXTERIOR: SPACE

Several TIE fighters approach the Death Star

Below: Matte painting, overlooking Mos Eisley, Peter Ellenshaw; facing page: sketch and production painting, Ralph McQuarrie

INTERIOR: DEATH STAR—CONTROL ROOM

VADER: Her resistance to the mind probe is considerable. It will be some time before we can extract any information from her.

An Imperial Officer interrupts the meeting.

IMPERIAL OFFICER: The final check-out is completed. All systems are operational. What course shall we set?

TARKIN: Perhaps she would respond to an alternative form of persuasion.

VADER: What do you mean?

TARKIN: I think it is time we demonstrated the full power of this station. (to soldier) Set your course for Princess Leia's home planet of Alderaan.

TROOPER: With pleasure.

EXTERIOR: TATOOINE—MOS EISLEY—STREET

Four heavily-armed stormtroopers move menacingly along a narrow slum alleyway crowded with darkly clad creatures hawking exotic goods in dingy little stalls. Men, monsters, and robots crouch in waste-filled doorways, whispering and hiding from the hot winds.

THREEPIO: Lock the door, Artoo.

One of the troopers checks a tightly locked door and moves on down the alleyway. The door slides open a crack and Threepio peeks out. Artoo is barely visible in the background.

TROOPER: All right, check that side of the street. It's secure. Move on to the next one.

The door opens, Threepio moves into the doorway.

THREEPIO: I would much rather have gone with Master Luke than stay here with you. I don't know what all this trouble is about, but I'm sure it must be your fault.

Artoo makes beeping sounds.

THREEPIO: You watch your language!

EXTERIOR: TATOOINE–MOS EISLEY–
STREET–ALLEYWAY–USED SPEEDER LOT

Ben and Luke are standing in a sleazy used speeder lot, talking with a tall, grotesque, insect-like used speeder dealer. Strange exotic bodies and spindly-legged beasts pass by as the insect concludes the sale by giving Luke some coins.

LUKE: He says it's the best he can do. Since the XP-38 came out, they just aren't in demand.

BEN: It will be enough.

Ben and Luke leave the speeder lot and walk down the dusty alleyway past a small robot herding a bunch of anteater-like creatures. Luke turns and gives one last forlorn look at his faithful speeder as he rounds a corner. A darkly clad creature moves out of the shadows as they pass and watches them as they disappear down another alley.

BEN: If the ship's as fast as he's boasting, we ought to do well.

INTERIOR: DOCKING BAY 94—DAY

Jabba the Hut and a half-dozen grisly alien pirates and purple creatures stand in the middle of the docking bay. Jabba is the grossest of the slavering hulks and his scarred face is a grim testimonial to his prowess as a vicious killer. He is a fat, slug-like creature with eyes on extended feelers and a huge ugly mouth.

JABBA: Come on out Solo!

A voice from directly behind the pirates startles them and they turn around to see Han Solo and the giant Wookiee, Chewbacca, standing behind them with no weapons in sight.

HAN: I've been waiting for you Jabba.

JABBA: I expected you would be.

Above: Early sketch of Chewbacca, Ralph McQuarrie; below: sketch of gun, Ralph McQuarrie

HAN: I'm not the type to run.
JABBA: (fatherly-smooth) Han, my boy, there are times when you disappoint me ... why haven't you paid me? And why did you have to fry poor Greedo like that ... after all we've been through together.
HAN: You sent Greedo to blast me.
JABBA: (mock surprise) Han, why you're the best smuggler in the business. You're too valuable to fry. He was only relaying my concern at your delays. He wasn't going to blast you.
HAN: I think he thought he was. Next time don't send one of those twerps. If you've got something to say to me, come see me yourself.
JABBA: Han, Han! If only you hadn't had to dump that shipment of spice ... you understand I just can't make an exception. Where would I be if every pilot who smuggled for me dumped their shipment at the first sign of an Imperial starship? It's not good business.
HAN: You know, even I get boarded sometimes, Jabba. I had no choice, but I've got a charter now and I can pay you back, plus a little extra. I just need some more time.
JABBA: (to his men) Put your blasters away. Han, my boy, I'm only doing this because you're the best and I need you. So, for an extra, say ... twenty percent I'll give you a little more time ... but this is it. If you disappoint me again, I'll put a price on your head so large you won't be able to go near a civilized system for the rest of your short life.

HAN: Jabba, I'll pay you because it's my pleasure.

EXTERIOR: DOCKING PORT ENTRY—ALLEYWAY

Chewbacca waits restlessly at the entrance to Docking Bay 94. Ben, Luke, and the robots make their way up the street. Chewbacca jabbers excitedly and signals for them to hurry. The darkly clad creature has followed them from the speeder lot. He stops in a nearby doorway and speaks into a small transmitter.

INTERIOR: MOS EISLEY SPACEPORT—DOCKING BAY 94

Chewbacca leads the group into the giant dirt pit that is Docking Bay 94. Resting in the middle of the huge hole is a large, round, beat-up, pieced-together hunk of junk that could only loosely be called a starship.
LUKE: What a piece of junk.
The tall figure of Han Solo comes down the boarding ramp.
HAN: She'll make point five beyond the speed of light. She may not look like much, but she's got it where it counts, kid. I've added some special modifications myself.
Luke scratches his head. It's obvious he isn't sure about all this. Chewbacca rushes up the ramp and urges the others to follow.
HAN: We're a little rushed, so if you'll hurry aboard we'll get out of here.
The group rushes up the gang plank, passing a grinning Han Solo.

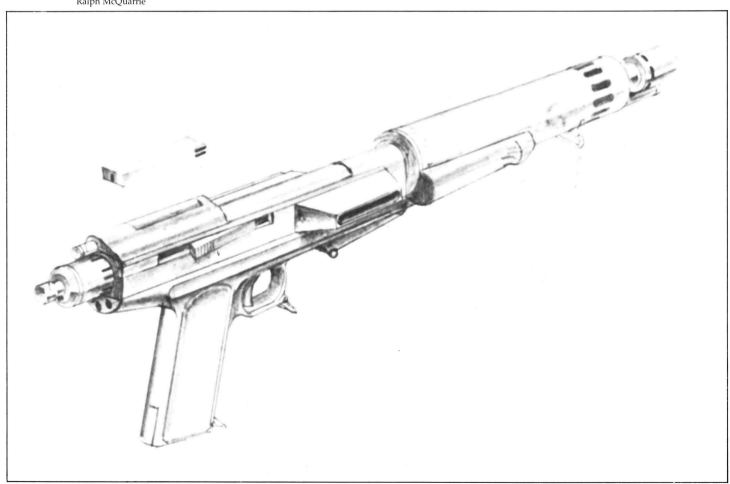

INTERIOR: MILLENNIUM FALCON

Chewbacca settles into the pilot's chair and starts the mighty engines of the starship.

INTERIOR: MOS EISLEY SPACEPORT—DOCKING BAY 94

Luke, Ben, Threepio, and Artoo move toward the Millennium Falcon passing Solo.
THREEPIO: Hello, sir.

EXTERIOR: TATOOINE. MOS EISLEY—STREET

Eight Imperial stormtroopers rush up to the darkly clad creature.
TROOPER: Which way?
The darkly clad creature points to the door of the docking bay.
TROOPER: All right, men. Load your weapons!

INTERIOR: MOS EISLEY SPACEPORT—DOCKING BAY 94

The troops hold their guns at the ready and charge down the docking bay entrance.
TROOPER: Stop that ship!
Han Solo looks up and sees the Imperial stormtroopers rushing into the docking bay. Several of the troopers fire at Han as he ducks into the spaceship.
TROOPER: Blast 'em!
Han draws his laser pistol and pops off a couple of shots which force the stormtroopers to dive for safety. The pirateship engines whine as Han hits the release button that slams the overhead entry shut.

INTERIOR: MILLENNIUM FALCON

HAN: Chewie, get us out of here!
The group straps in for takeoff.
THREEPIO: Oh, my. I'd forgotten how much I hate space travel.

EXTERIOR: TATOOINE—MOS EISLEY—STREETS

The half-dozen stormtroopers at a check point hear the general alarm and look to the sky as the huge starship rises above the dingy slum dwellings and quickly disappears into the morning sky.

INTERIOR: MILLENNIUM FALCON—CABIN

Han climbs into the pilot's chair next to Chewbacca, who chatters away as he points to something on the radar scope.

EXTERIOR: SPACE—PLANET TATOOINE

The Corellian pirateship zooms from Tatooine into space.

INTERIOR: MILLENNIUM FALCON—COCKPIT

Han frantically types information into the ship's computer. Little Artoo appears momentarily at the cockpit doorway, makes a few beeping remarks, then scurries away.
HAN: It looks like an Imperial cruiser. Our passengers must be hotter than I thought. Try and hold them off. Angle the deflector shield while I make the calculations for the jump to light speed.

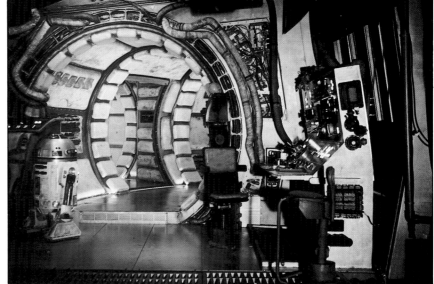

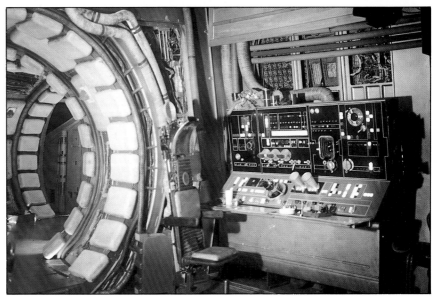

Photographs of Millennium Falcon interior, John Jay

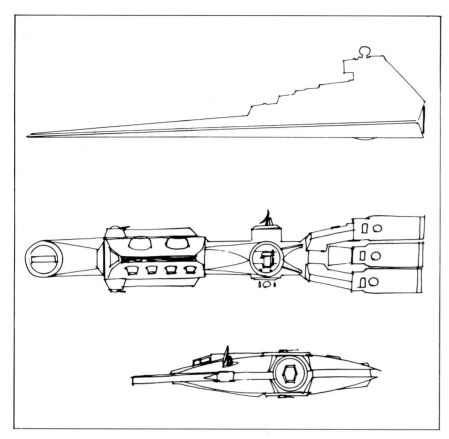

Above: Chart showing relative size of spacecraft, Joe Johnston

Opposite page: Composite photograph; matte painting of Tatooine, Ralph McQuarrie; photograph of Millennium Falcon model, Richard Edlund; airbrushing, Ron Larson

EXTERIOR: SPACE—PLANET TATOOINE

The Millennium Falcon pirateship races away from the yellow planet, Tatooine. It is followed by two huge Imperial Stardestroyers.

INTERIOR: MILLENNIUM FALCON—COCKPIT

Over the shoulders of Chewbacca and Han, we can see the galaxy spread before them. Luke and Ben make their way into the cramped cockpit where Han continues his calculation.

HAN: Stay sharp! There are two more coming in; they're going to try to cut us off.

LUKE: Why don't you outrun them? I thought you said this thing was fast.

HAN: Watch your mouth, kid, or you're going to find yourself floating home. We'll be safe enough once we make the jump to hyperspace. Besides, I know a few maneuvers. We'll lose them!

EXTERIOR: SPACE—PLANET TATOOINE

Imperial cruisers fire at the pirateship.

INTERIOR: MILLENNIUM FALCON—COCKPIT

The ship shudders as an explosion flashes outside the window.

HAN: Here's where the fun begins!

BEN: How long before you can make the jump to light speed?

HAN: It'll take a few moments to get the coordinates from the navi-computer.

The ship begins to rock violently as lasers hit it.

LUKE: Are you kidding? At the rate they're gaining...

HAN: Traveling through hyperspace isn't like dusting crops, boy! Without precise calculations we could fly right through a star or bounce too close to a supernova and that'd end your trip real quick, wouldn't it?

The ship is now constantly battered with laserfire as a red warning light begins to flash.

LUKE: What's that flashing?

HAN: We're losing our deflector shield. Go strap yourself in, I'm going to make the jump to light speed.

The galaxy brightens and they move faster, almost as if crashing a barrier. Stars become streaks as the pirateship makes the jump to hyperspace.

EXTERIOR: SPACE

The Millennium Falcon zooms into infinity in less than a second.

EXTERIOR: DEATH STAR

Alderaan looms behind the Death Star battlestation.

INTERIOR: DEATH STAR—CONTROL ROOM

Admiral Motti enters the quiet control room and bows before Governor Tarkin, who stands before the huge wall screen displaying a small green planet.

MOTTI: We've entered the Alderaan system.

Vader and two stormtroopers enter with Princess Leia. Her hands are bound.

LEIA: Governor Tarkin, I should have expected to find you holding Vader's leash. I recognized your foul stench when I was brought on board.

TARKIN: Charming to the last. You don't know how hard I found it signing the order to terminate your life!

LEIA: I'm surprised you had the courage to take the responsibility yourself!

TARKIN: Princess Leia, before your execution I would like you to be my guest at a ceremony that will make this battle station operational. No star system will dare oppose the Emperor now.

LEIA: The more you tighten your grip, Tarkin, the more star systems will slip through your fingers.

TARKIN: Not after we demonstrate the power of this station. In a way, you have determined the choice of the planet that'll be destroyed first. Since you are reluctant to provide us with the location of the Rebel base, I have chosen to test this station's destructive power... on your home planet of Alderaan.

LEIA: No! Alderaan is peaceful. We have no weapons. You can't possibly...

TARKIN: You would prefer another target? A military target? Then name the system!

Tarkin waves menacingly toward Leia.

TARKIN: I grow tired of asking this. So it'll be the last time. Where is the Rebel base?

Leia overhears an intercom voice announcing the approach to Alderaan.

LEIA: (softly) Dantooine.

Leia lowers her head.

LEIA: They're on Dantooine.

TARKIN: There. You see, Lord Vader, she can be reasonable. (addressing Motti) Continue with the operation. You may fire when ready.

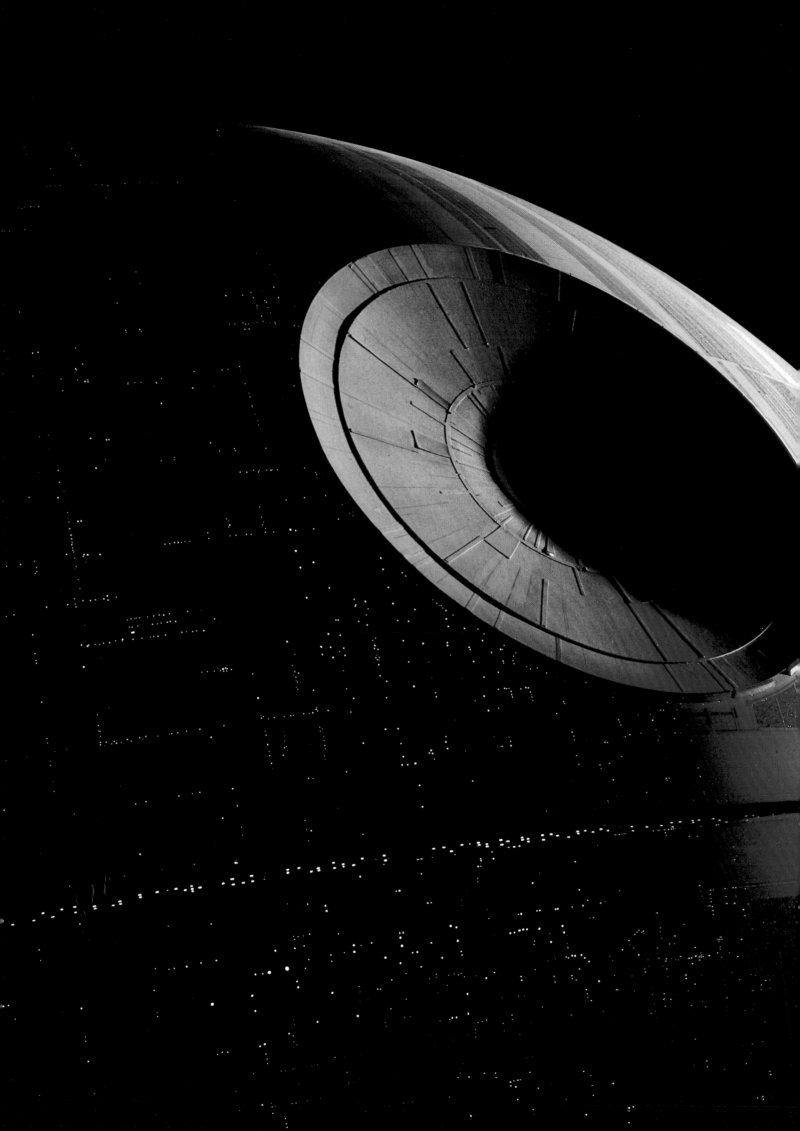

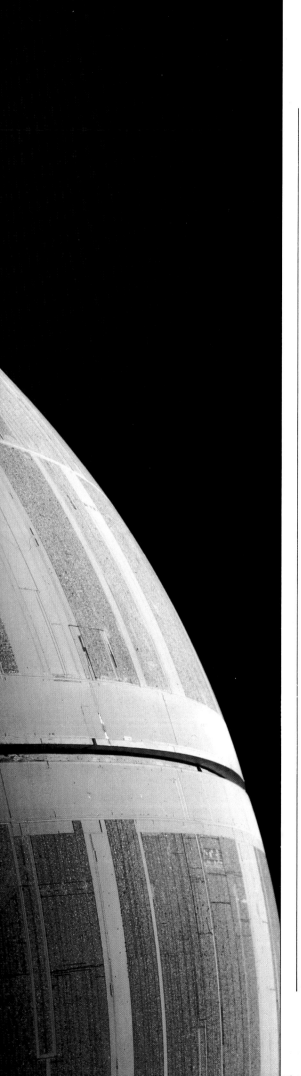

LEIA: What?

TARKIN: You're far too trusting. Dantooine is too remote to make an effective demonstration. But don't worry. We will deal with your Rebel friends soon enough.

LEIA: No!

Opposite page: Photograph of Death Star model, Richard Edlund; above: matte painting, Ralph McQuarrie

INTERIOR: DEATH STAR—BLAST CHAMBER

VADER: Commence primary ignition.

A button is pressed which switches on a panel of lights. A hooded Imperial soldier reaches overhead and pulls a lever. Another lever is pulled. Vader reaches for still another lever and a bank of lights on a panel and wall light up. A huge beam of light emanates from within a cone-shaped area and converges into a single laser beam out toward Alderaan. The small green planet of Alderaan is blown into space dust.

INTERIOR: MILLENNIUM FALCON—CENTRAL HOLD AREA

Ben watches as Luke practices the lightsaber with a small "seeker" robot. Ben suddenly turns away and sits down. He falters, seems almost faint.

LUKE: Are you all right? What's wrong?

BEN: I felt a great disturbance in the Force...as if millions of voices suddenly cried out in terror and were suddenly silenced. I fear something terrible has happened.

Ben rubs his forehead. He seems to drift into a trance. Then he fixes his gaze on Luke.

BEN: You'd better get on with your exercises.

Han Solo enters the room.

HAN: Well, you can forget your troubles with those Imperial slugs. I told you I'd outrun 'em.

Luke is once again practicing with the lightsaber.

HAN: Don't everybody thank me at once.

Threepio watches Chewbacca and Artoo who are engrossed in a game in which three-dimensional holographic figures move along a chess-type board.

HAN: Anyway, we should be at Alderaan about oh-two-hundred hours.

Chewbacca and the two robots sit around the lighted table covered with small holographic monsters. Each side of the table has a small computer monitor embedded in it. Chewbacca seems very pleased with himself as he rests his lanky fur-covered arms over his head.

THREEPIO: Now be careful, Artoo.

Artoo immediately reaches up and taps the computer with his stubby claw hand, causing one of the holographic creatures to walk to the new square. A sudden frown crosses Chewbacca's face and he begins yelling gibberish at the tiny robot. Threepio intercedes on behalf of his small companion and begins to argue with the huge Wookiee.

THREEPIO: He made a fair move. Screaming about it won't help you.

HAN: (interrupting) Let him have it. It's not wise to upset a Wookiee.

THREEPIO: But sir, nobody worries about upsetting a droid.

HAN: That's 'cause droids don't pull people's arms out of their sockets when they lose. Wookiees are known to do that.

THREEPIO: I see your point, sir. I suggest a new strategy, Artoo. Let the Wookiee win.

Luke stands in the middle of the small hold area; he seems frozen in place. A humming lightsaber is held high over his head. Ben watches him from the corner, studying his movements. Han watches with a bit of smugness.

BEN: Remember, a Jedi can feel the Force flowing through him.

LUKE: You mean it controls your actions?

BEN: Partially. But it also obeys your commands.

Suspended at eye level, about ten feet in front of Luke, a "seeker," a chrome baseball-like robot covered with antennae, hovers slowly in a wide arc. The ball floats to one side of the youth then to the other. Suddenly it makes a lightning-swift lunge and stops within a few feet of Luke's face. Luke doesn't move and the ball backs off. It slowly moves behind the boy, then makes another quick lunge, this time emitting a blood red laser beam as it attacks. It hits Luke in the leg causing him to tumble over. Han lets loose with a burst of laughter.

HAN: Hokey religions and ancient weapons are no match for a good blaster at your side, kid.

LUKE: You don't believe in the Force, do you?

HAN: Kid, I've flown from one side of this galaxy to the other. I've seen a lot of strange stuff, but I've never seen anything to make me believe there's one all-powerful force controlling everything. There's no mystical energy field that controls my destiny.

Ben smiles quietly.

HAN: It's all a lot of simple tricks and nonsense.

BEN: I suggest you try it again, Luke.

Ben places a large helmet on Luke's head which covers his eyes.

BEN: This time, let go of your conscious self and act on instinct.

LUKE: (laughing) With the blast shield down, I can't even see. How am I supposed to fight?

BEN: Your eyes can deceive you. Don't trust them.

Han skeptically shakes his head as Ben throws the seeker into the air. The ball shoots straight up in the air, then drops like a rock. Luke swings the lightsaber around blindly missing the seeker, which fires off a laserbolt which hits Luke square on the seat of the pants. He lets out a painful yell and attempts to hit the seeker.

BEN: Stretch out with your feelings.

Luke stands in one place, seemingly frozen. The seeker makes a dive at Luke and, incredibly, he manages to deflect the bolt. The ball ceases firing and moves back to its original position.

BEN: You see, you can do it.

HAN: I call it luck.

BEN: In my experience, there's no such thing as luck.

HAN: Look, going good against remotes is one thing. Going good against the living? That's something else.

Solo notices a small light flashing on the far side of the control panel.

HAN: Looks like we're coming up on Alderaan.

Han and Chewbacca head back to the cockpit.

LUKE: You know, I did feel something. I could almost see the remote.

Below: Storyboard, Gary Myers, Paul Huston, Steve Gawley, Ronnie Shepherd; under direction of Joe Johnston

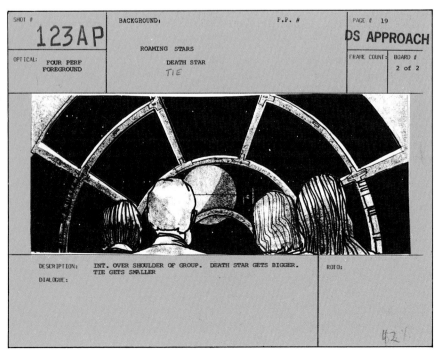

SHOT # 123AP	BACKGROUND: ROAMING STARS	P.P. #	PAGE # 19 DS APPROACH
OPTICAL: FOUR PERF FOREGROUND	DEATH STAR TIE		FRAME COUNT: BOARD # 2 of 2

DESCRIPTION: INT. OVER SHOULDER OF GROUP. DEATH STAR GETS BIGGER. TIE GETS SMALLER	ROTO:
DIALOGUE:	

BEN: That's good. You have taken your first step into a large world.

INTERIOR: DEATH STAR—CONFERENCE ROOM

Imperial Officer Cass stands before Governor Tarkin and the evil Dark Lord Darth Vader.
TARKIN: Yes.
OFFICER CASS: Our scout ships have reached Dantooine. They found the remains of a Rebel base, but they estimate that it has been deserted for some time. They are now conducting an extensive search of the surrounding systems.
TARKIN: She lied! She lied to us!
VADER: I told you she would never consciously betray the Rebellion.
TARKIN: Terminate her...immediately!

EXTERIOR: HYPERSPACE

The pirateship is just coming out of hyperspace; a strange surreal light show surrounds the ship.

INTERIOR: MILLENNIUM FALCON—COCKPIT

HAN: Stand by, Chewie, here we go. Cut in the sublight engines.
Han pulls back on a control lever. Outside the cockpit window stars begin streaking past, seem to decrease in speed, then stop. Suddenly the starship begins to shudder and violently shake about. Asteroids begin to race toward them, battering the sides of the ship.
HAN: What the...? Aw, we've come out of hyperspace into a meteor shower. Some kind of asteroid collision. It's not on any of the charts.
The giant Wookiee flips off several controls and seems very cool in the emergency. Luke makes his way into the bouncing cockpit.
LUKE: What's going on?
HAN: Our position is correct, except...no, Alderaan!
LUKE: What do you mean? Where is it?
HAN: That's what I'm trying to tell you, kid. It ain't there. It's been totally blown away.
LUKE: What? How?
Ben moves into the cockpit behind Luke as the ship begins to settle down.
BEN: Destroyed...by the Empire!
HAN: The entire starfleet couldn't destroy the whole planet. It'd take a thousand ships with more fire power than I've...
A signal light starts flashing on the control panel and a muffled alarm starts humming.
HAN: There's another ship coming in.
LUKE: Maybe they know what happened.
BEN: It's an Imperial fighter.
Chewbacca barks his concern. A huge explosion bursts outside the cockpit window, shaking the ship violently. A tiny, finned Imperial TIE fighter races past the cockpit window.
LUKE: It followed us!
BEN: No. It's a short range fighter.
HAN: There aren't any bases around here. Where did it come from?

EXTERIOR: SPACE

The fighter races past the Corellian pirateship.

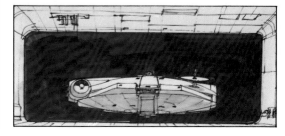

Left: Storyboards,
Gary Myers, Paul Huston, Steve
Gawley, Ronnie Shepherd; under
direction of Joe Johnston

Above: Storyboard, Alex
Tavoularis; right: Matte painting,
Death Star surface,
Ralph McQuarrie

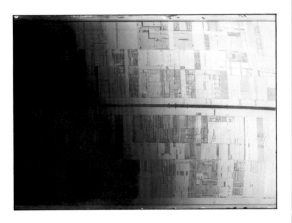

INTERIOR: MILLENNIUM FALCON—COCKPIT

LUKE: It sure is leaving in a big hurry. If they identify us, we're in big trouble.
HAN: Not if I can help it. Chewie . . . jam its transmissions.
BEN: It'd be as well to let it go. It's too far out of range.
HAN: Not for long . . .

EXTERIOR: SPACE

The pirateship zooms over the camera and away into the vastness of space after the Imperial TIE fighter.

INTERIOR: MILLENNIUM FALCON—COCKPIT

The tension mounts as the pirate ship gains on the tiny fighter. In the distance, one of the stars becomes brighter until it is obvious that the TIE ship is heading for it. Ben stands behind Chewbacca.
BEN: A fighter that size couldn't get this deep into space on its own.
LUKE: Then he must have gotten lost, been part of a convoy or something . . .
HAN: Well, he ain't going to be around long enough to tell anyone about us.

EXTERIOR: SPACE

The TIE fighter is losing ground to the larger pirateship as they race toward camera and disappear overhead.

INTERIOR: MILLENNIUM FALCON—COCKPIT
The distant star can now be distinguished as a small moon or planet.
LUKE: Look at him. He's heading for that small moon.

Right: storyboard, Alex
Tavoularis; below and opposite
page: production paintings,
Ralph McQuarrie

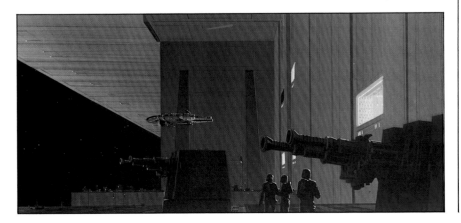

HAN: I think I can get him before he gets there... he's almost in range.

The small moon begins to take on the appearance of a monstrous spherical battle station.

BEN: That's not a moon! It's space station.

HAN: It's too big to be a space station.

LUKE: I have a very bad feeling about this.

BEN: Turn the ship around!

HAN: Yeah, I think you're right. Full reverse! Chewie, lock in the auxiliary power.

The pirateship shudders and the TIE fighter accelerates away toward the gargantuan battle station.

LUKE: Why are we still moving towards it?

HAN: We're caught in a tractor beam! It's pulling us in.

LUKE: But there's gotta be something you can do!

HAN: There's nothin' I can do about it, kid. I'm in full power. I'm going to have to shut down. But they're not going to get me without a fight!

Ben Kenobi puts a hand on his shoulder.

BEN: You can't win. But there are alternatives to fighting.

INTERIOR: MILLENNIUM FALCON—DEATH STAR

As the battered pirate starship is towed closer to the awesome metal moon, the immense size of the massive battle station becomes staggering. Running along the equator of the gigantic sphere is a mile-high band of huge docking ports into which the helpless pirateship is dragged.

EXTERIOR: DEATH STAR—HUGE PORT DOORS

The helpless Millennium Falcon is pulled past a docking port control room and huge laser turret cannons.

VOICE OVER DEATH STAR INTERCOM: Clear Bay twenty-three-seven. We are opening the magnetic field.

INTERIOR: DEATH STAR—DOCKING BAY 2037

The pirateship is pulled in through port doors of the Death Star, coming to rest in a huge hangar. Thirty stormtroopers stand at attention in a central assembly area.

OFFICER: To your stations!

OFFICER: (to another officer) Come with me.

INTERIOR: DEATH STAR—HALLWAY

Stormtroopers run to their posts.

INTERIOR: DEATH STAR—HANGAR 2037

A line of stormtroopers march toward the pirateship in readiness to board it, while other troopers stand with weapons ready to fire.

OFFICER: Close all outboard shields! Close all outboard shields!

Sketch, John Barry

INTERIOR: DEATH STAR—CONFERENCE ROOM

Tarkin pushes a button and responds to intercom buzz.
TARKIN: Yes.
VOICE: (over intercom) We've captured a freighter entering the remains of the Alderaan system. Its markings match those of a ship that blasted its way out of Mos Eisley.
VADER: They must be trying to return the stolen plans to the princess. She may yet be of some use to us.

INTERIOR: DEATH STAR—DOCKING BAY 2037

Vader and a commander approach the troops as an Officer and several heavily armed troops exit the spacecraft.
VOICE: (over intercom) Unlock one-five-seven and nine. Release charges.
OFFICER: (to Vader) There's no one on board sir. According to the log, the crew abandoned ship right after takeoff. It must be a decoy, sir. Several of the escape pods have been jettisoned.
VADER: Did you find any droids?
OFFICER: No, sir. If there were any on board, they must also have jettisoned.
VADER: Send a scanning crew on board. I want every part of this ship checked.
OFFICER: Yes, sir.
VADER: I sense something... a presence I haven't felt since...
Vader turns quickly and exits the hangar.
OFFICER: Get me a scanning crew in here on the double. I want every part of this ship checked!

INTERIOR: MILLENNIUM FALCON—HALLWAY

A trooper runs through the hallway heading for the exit. In a few moments all is quiet. The muffled sounds of a distant officer giving orders finally fade. Two floor panels suddenly pop up revealing Han Solo and Luke. Ben Kenobi sticks his head out of a third locker.
LUKE: Boy, it's lucky you had these compartments.
HAN: I use them for smuggling. I never thought I'd be smuggling myself in them. This is ridiculous. Even if I could take off, I'd never get past the tractor beam.
BEN: Leave that to me!
HAN: Damn fool. I knew that you were going to say that!
BEN: Who's the more foolish... the fool or the fool who follows him?
Han shakes his head, muttering to himself. Chewbacca agrees.

INTERIOR: DEATH STAR—MAIN FORWARD BAY

The two crewmen carry a heavy box on board the ship, past the two stormtroopers guarding either side of the ramp.
TROOPER: The ship's all yours. If the scanners pick up anything, report it immediately. All right, let's go.
The crewmen enter the pirateship and a loud crashing sound is followed by a voice calling to the guard below.
HAN'S VOICE: Hey down there, could you give us a hand with this?
The stormtroopers enter the ship and a quick round of gunfire is heard.

INTERIOR: DEATH STAR—FORWARD BAY—COMMAND OFFICE

In a very small command office near the entrance to the pirateship, a Gantry Officer looks out his window and notices the guards are missing. He speaks into the comlink.
GANTRY OFFICER: TX-four-two-one. Why aren't you at your post? TX-four-two-one, do you copy?
A stormtrooper comes down the ramp of the pirateship and waves to the gantry officer, pointing to his ear indicating his comlink is not working. The gantry officer shakes his head in disgust and heads for the door, giving his aide an annoyed look.
GANTRY OFFICER: Take over. We've got a bad transmitter. I'll see what I can do.
As the officer approaches the door, it slides open revealing the towering Chewbacca. The gantry officer, in a momentary state of shock, stumbles backward. With a bone-chilling howl, the giant Wookiee flattens the officer with one blow. The aide immediately reaches for his pistol, but is blasted by Han, dressed as an Imperial stormtrooper. Ben and the robots enter the room quickly followed by Luke, also dressed as a stormtrooper. Luke quickly removes his helmet.
LUKE: You know, between his howling and your blasting everything in sight, it's a wonder the whole station doesn't know we're here.
HAN: Bring them on! I prefer a straight fight to all this sneaking around.
THREEPIO: We found the computer outlet, sir.
Ben feeds some information into the computer and a map of the city appears on the monitor. He begins to inspect it carefully. Threepio and Artoo look over the control panel. Artoo finds something that makes him whistle wildly.
BEN: Plug in. He should be able to interpret the entire Imperial computer network.
Artoo punches his claw arm into the computer socket and the vast Imperial brain network comes to life, feeding information to the little robot. After a few moments, he beeps something.
THREEPIO: He says he's found the main control to the power beam that's holding the ship here. He'll try to make the precise location appear on the monitor.
The computer monitor flashes readouts.
THREEPIO: The tractor beam is coupled to the main reactor in seven locations. A power loss at one of the terminals will allow the ship to leave.
Ben studies the data on the monitor readout.
BEN: I don't think you boys can help. I must go alone.
HAN: Whatever you say. I've done more than I bargained for on this trip already.
LUKE: I want to go with you.
BEN: Be patient, Luke. Stay and watch over the droids.
LUKE: But he can...
BEN: They must be delivered safely or other star systems will suffer the same fate as Alderaan. Your destiny lies along a different path from mine. The Force will be with you... always!
Ben adjusts the lightsaber on his belt and silently steps out of the command office, then disappears down a long grey hallway. Chewbacca barks a comment and Han shakes his head in agreement.

Below: Matte paintings of Millennium Falcon in Death Star, Peter Ellenshaw

Left: Frame enlargement from
Star Wars

Left: Matte painting,
Peter Ellenshaw

HAN: Boy, you said it, Chewie.
Han looks at Luke.
HAN: Where did you dig up that old fossil?
LUKE: Ben is a great man.
HAN: Yeah, great at getting us into trouble.
LUKE: I didn't hear you give any ideas...
HAN: Well, anything would be better than just hanging around waiting for them to pick us up...
LUKE: Who do you think...
Suddenly Artoo begins to whistle and beep a blue streak. Luke goes over to him.
LUKE: What is it?
THREEPIO: I'm afraid I'm not quite sure, sir. He says "I found her," and keeps repeating, "She's here."
LUKE: Well, who... who has he found?

Artoo whistles a frantic reply.
THREEPIO: Princess Leia.
LUKE: The princess? She's here?
HAN: Princess?
LUKE: Where... where is she?
HAN: Princess? What's going on?
THREEPIO: Level five. Detention block AA-twenty-three. I'm afraid she's scheduled to be terminated.
LUKE: Oh, no! We've got to do something.
HAN: What are you talking about?
LUKE: The droid belongs to her. She's the one in the message. We've got to help her.
HAN: Now, look, don't get any funny ideas. The old man wants us to wait right here.

Below: Matte painting, Peter Ellenshaw

LUKE: But he didn't know she was here. Look, will you just find a way back into that detention block?
HAN: I'm not going anywhere.
LUKE: They're going to execute her. Look, a few minutes ago you said you didn't want to just wait here to be captured. Now all you want to do is stay.
HAN: Marching into the detention area is not what I had in mind.
LUKE: But they're going to kill her!
HAN: Better her than me...
LUKE: She's rich.
Chewbacca growls.
HAN: Rich?
LUKE: Yes. Rich, powerful! Listen, if you were to rescue her, the reward would be...

HAN: What?
LUKE: Well, more wealth than you can imagine.
HAN: I don't know, I can imagine quite a bit!
LUKE: You'll get it!
HAN: I'd better!
LUKE: You will...
HAN: All right, kid. But you'd better be right about this!
Han looks at Chewie, who grunts a short grunt.
LUKE: All right.
HAN: What's your plan?
LUKE: Uh...Threepio, hand me those binders there will you?
Luke moves toward Chewbacca with electronic cuffs.
LUKE: Okay. Now, I'm going to put these on you.

Below: Matte painting for swing across scene, Peter Ellenshaw

Chewie lets out a hideous growl.
LUKE: Okay. Han, you put these on.
Luke sheepishly hands the binders to Han.
HAN: Don't worry, Chewie. I think I know what he has in mind.
The Wookiee has a worried and frightened look on his face as Han binds him with electronics cuffs.
THREEPIO: Master Luke, sir! Pardon me for asking...but, ah...what should Artoo and I do if we're discovered here?
LUKE: Lock the door!
HAN: And hope they don't have blasters.
THREEPIO: That isn't very reassuring.
Luke and Han put on their armored stormtrooper helmets and start off into the giant Imperial Death Star.

INTERIOR: DEATH STAR—DETENTION AREA—ELEVATOR TUBE

Han and Luke try to look inconspicuous in their armored suits as they wait for a vacuum elevator to arrive. Troops, bureaucrats, and robots bustle about, ignoring the trio completely. Only a few give the giant Wookiee a curious glance.
Finally a small elevator arrives and the trio enters.
LUKE: I can't see a thing in this helmet.
A bureaucrat races to get aboard also, but is signaled away by Han. The door to the pod-like vehicle slides closed and the elevator car takes off through a vacuum tube.

INTERIOR: DEATH STAR—MAIN HALLWAY

Several Imperial officers walk through the wide main passageway. They pass several stormtroopers and a robot similar to Threepio but with an insect face. At the far end of the hallway, a passing flash of Ben Kenobi appears, then disappears down a small hallway. His appearance is so fleeting that it is hard to tell if he is real or just an illusion. No one in the hallway seems to notice him.

INTERIOR: DEATH STAR—INTERIOR
ELEVATOR—DETENTION SECURITY AREA

Luke and Han step forward to exit the elevator, but the door slides open behind them. The giant Wookiee and his two guards enter the old grey security station. Guards and laser gates are everywhere. Han whispers to Luke under his breath.
HAN: This is not going to work.
LUKE: Why didn't you say so before?
HAN: I did say so before!

INTERIOR: DETENTION AREA
Elevator doors open. A tall, grim looking Officer approaches the trio.
OFFICER: Where are you taking this...thing?
Chewie growls a bit at the remark but Han nudges him to shut up.
LUKE: Prisoner transfer from Block one-one-three-eight.
OFFICER: I wasn't notified. I'll have to clear it.
The officer goes back to his console and begins to punch in the information. There are only three other troopers in the area. Luke and Han survey the situation, checking all of the alarms, laser gates, and camera eyes. Han unfastens one of Chewbacca's electronic cuffs and shrugs to Luke.
Suddenly Chewbacca throws up his hands and lets out

with one of his ear-piercing howls. He grabs Han's laser rifle.
HAN: Look out! He's loose!
LUKE: He's going to pull us all apart!
HAN: Go get him!
The startled guards are momentarily dumbfounded. Luke and Han have already pulled out their laser pistols and are blasting away at the terrifying Wookiee. Their barrage of laserfire misses Chewbacca, but hits the camera eyes, laser gate controls, and the Imperial guards. The officer is the last of the guards to fall under the laserfire just as he is about to push the alarm system. Han rushes to the comlink system, which is screeching questions about what is going on. He quickly checks the computer readout.
HAN: We've got to find out which cell this princess of yours is in. Here it is... cell twenty-one-eight-seven. You go get her. I'll hold them here.
Luke races down one of the cell corridors. Han speaks into the buzzing comlink.
HAN: (sounding official) Everything is under control. Situation normal.
INTERCOM VOICE: What happened?
HAN: (getting nervous) Uh...had a slight weapons malfunction. But, uh, everything's perfectly all right now. We're fine. We're all fine here, now, thank you. How are you?
INTERCOM VOICE: We're sending a squad up.
HAN: Uh, uh, negative, negative. We had a reactor leak here now. Give us a few minutes to lock it down. Large leak...very dangerous.
INTERCOM VOICE: Who is this? What's your operating number?
Han blasts the comlink and it explodes.
HAN: Boring conversation anyway. (yelling down the hall) Luke! We're going to have company!

INTERIOR: DEATH STAR—CELL ROW

Luke stops in front of one of the cells and blasts the door away with his laser pistol. When the smoke clears, Luke sees the dazzling young princess-senator. She had been sleeping and is now looking at him with an uncomprehending look on her face. Luke is stunned by her incredible beauty and stands staring at her with his mouth hanging open.
LEIA: (finally) Aren't you a little short for a stormtrooper?
Luke takes off his helmet, coming out of it.
LUKE: What? Oh... the uniform. I'm Luke Skywalker. I'm here to rescue you.
LEIA: You're who?
LUKE: I'm here to rescue you. I've got your R2 unit. I'm here with Ben Kenobi.
LEIA: Ben Kenobi is here! Where is he?
LUKE. Come on!

INTERIOR: DEATH STAR—CONFERENCE ROOM

Darth Vader paces the room as Governor Tarkin sits at the far end of the conference table.
VADER: He is here...
TARKIN: Obi-Wan Kenobi! What makes you think so?
VADER: A tremor in the Force. The last time I felt it was in the presence of my old master.
TARKIN: Surely he must be dead by now.
VADER: Don't underestimate the Force.

Below: Sketch of a prisoner, John Mollo

TARKIN: The Jedi are extinct, their fire has gone out of the universe. You, my friend, are all that's left of their religion.

There is a quiet buzz on the comlink.

TARKIN: Yes.

INTERCOM VOICE: Governor Tarkin, we have an emergency alert in detention block AA-twenty-three.

TARKIN: The princess! Put all sections on alert!

VADER: Obi-Wan *is* here. The Force is with him.

TARKIN: If you're right, he must not be allowed to escape.

VADER: Escape may not be his plan. I must face him alone.

INTERIOR: DEATH STAR—DETENTION AREA—HALLWAY

An ominous buzzing sound is heard on the other side of the elevator door.

HAN: Chewie!

Chewbacca responds with a growling noise.

HAN: Get behind me! Get behind me!

A series of explosions knocks a hole in the elevator door through which several Imperial troops begin to emerge.

Han and Chewie fire their laser pistols at them through the smoke and flames. They turn and run down the cell hallway, meeting up with Luke and Leia rushing toward them.

HAN: Can't get out that way.

LEIA: Looks like you managed to cut off our only escape route.

HAN: (sarcastically) Maybe you'd like it back in your cell, Your Highness.

Luke takes a small comlink transmitter from his belt as they continue to exchange fire with stormtroopers making their way down the corridor.

LUKE: See-Threepio! See-Threepio!

THREEPIO: (over comlink) Yes sir?

LUKE: We've been cut off! Are there any other ways out of the cell bay?...What was that? I didn't copy!

INTERIOR: DEATH STAR—MAIN BAY GANTRY—CONTROL TOWER

Threepio paces the control center as little Artoo beeps and whistles a blue streak. Threepio yells into the small comlink transmitter.

THREEPIO: I said, all systems have been alerted to your presence, sir. The main entrance seems to be the only way in or out; all other information on your level is restricted.

Someone begins banging on the door.

TROOPER VOICE: Open up in there!

THREEPIO: Oh, no!

INTERIOR: DEATH STAR—DETENTION CORRIDOR

Luke and Leia crouch together in an alcove for protection as they continue to exchange fire with troops. Han and Chewbacca are barely able to keep the stormtroopers at bay at the far end of the hallway. The laserfire is very intense, and smoke fills the narrow cell corridor.

LUKE: There isn't any other way out.

HAN: I can't hold them off forever! Now what?

LEIA: This is some rescue. When you came in here, didn't you have a plan for getting out?

HAN: (pointing to Luke) He is the brains, sweetheart.

Luke manages a sheepish grin and shrugs his shoulders.

LUKE: Well, I didn't...

The Princess grabs Luke's gun and fires at a small grate in the wall next to Han, almost frying him.

HAN: What the hell are you doing?

LEIA: Somebody has to save our skins. Into the garbage chute, wise guy.

She jumps through the narrow opening as Han and Chewbacca look on in amazement. Chewbacca sniffs the garbage chute and says something.

HAN: Get in there you big furry oaf! I don't care what you smell! Get in there and don't worry about it.

Han gives him a big kick and the Wookiee disappears into the tiny opening. Luke and Han continue firing as they work their way toward the opening.

HAN: Wonderful girl! Either I'm going to kill her or I'm beginning to like her. Get in there!

Luke ducks laserfire as he jumps into the darkness. Han fires off a couple of quick blasts creating a smokey cover, then slides into the chute himself and is gone.

INTERIOR: DEATH STAR—GARBAGE ROOM

Han tumbles into a large room filled with garbage and muck. Luke is already stumbling around looking for an

Left: Production painting, Ralph McQuarrie; below: Imperial crewman and pilot costume sketches, John Mollo

exit. He finds a small hatchway and struggles to get it open. It won't budge.

HAN: (sarcastically) Oh! The garbage chute was a really wonderful idea. What an incredible smell you've discovered! Let's get out of here! Get away from there...

LUKE: No! Wait!

Han draws his laser pistol and fires at the hatch. The laserbolt ricochets wildly around the small metal room. Everyone dives for cover in the garbage as the bolt explodes almost on top of them. Leia climbs out of the garbage with a rather grim look on her face.

LUKE: Will you forget it? I already tried it. It's magnetically sealed!

LEIA: Put that thing away! You're going to get us all killed.

HAN: Absolutely, Your Worship. Look, I had everything under control until you led us down here. You know, it's not going to take them long to figure out what happened to us.

LEIA: It could be worse...

A loud, horrible, inhuman moan works its way up from the murky depths. Chewbacca lets out a terrified howl and begins to back away. Han and Luke stand fast with their laser pistols drawn. The Wookiee is cowering near one of the walls.

HAN: It's worse.

LUKE: There's something alive in here!

HAN: That's your imagination.

LUKE: Something just moved past my leg! Look! Did you see that?

HAN: What?

LUKE: Help!

Suddenly Luke is yanked under the garbage.

HAN: Luke! Luke! Luke!

Solo tries to get to Luke. Luke surfaces with a gasp of air and thrashing of limbs. A membrane tentacle is wrapped around his throat.

LEIA: Luke!

Leia extends a long pipe toward him.

LEIA: Luke, Luke, grab a hold of this.

LUKE: Blast it, will you! My gun's jammed.

HAN: Where?

LUKE: Anywhere. Oh!!

Solo fires his gun downward. Luke is pulled back into the muck by the slimy tentacle.

HAN: Luke! Luke!

Suddenly the walls of the garbage receptacle shudder and move in a couple of inches. Then everything is deathly quiet. Han and Leia give each other a worried look as Chewbacca howls in the corner. With a rush of bubbles and muck Luke suddenly bobs to the surface.

LEIA: Grab him!

Luke seems to be released by the thing.

LEIA: What happened?

LUKE: I don't know, it just let go of me and disappeared...

HAN: I've got a very bad feeling about this.

Before anyone can say anything the walls begin to rumble and edge toward the Rebels.

LUKE: The walls are moving!

LEIA: Don't just stand there. Try and brace it with something.

They place poles and long metal beams between the closing walls, but they are simply snapped and bent as the giant trashmasher rumbles on. The situation doesn't look too good.

Right: Photograph of Death Star detention corridor set; below: sketches of Death Star trench, Ralph McQuarrie

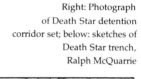

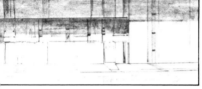

LUKE: Wait a minute!

Luke pulls out his comlink.

LUKE: Threepio! Come in Threepio! Threepio! Where could he be?

INTERIOR: DEATH STAR—MAIN GANTRY—COMMAND OFFICE

A soft buzzer and the muted voice of Luke calling out for See-Threepio can be heard on Threepio's hand comlink, which is siting on the deserted computer console. Artoo and Threepio are nowhere in sight. Suddenly there is a great explosion and the door of the control tower flies across the floor. Four armed stormtroopers enter the chamber.

FIRST TROOPER: Take over! (pointing to a dead officer) See to him! Look there!

A trooper pushes a button and the supply cabinet door slides open. See-Threepio and Artoo-Detoo are inside.

Artoo follows his bronze companion out into the office.

THREEPIO: They're madmen! They're heading for the prison level. If you hurry, you might catch them.

FIRST OFFICER: (to his troops) Follow me!

You stand guard.

The troops hustle off down the hallway, leaving Guard to watch over the command office.

THREEPIO: (to Artoo) Come on!

The guard aims a blaster at them.

THREEPIO: Oh! All this excitement has overrun the circuits in my counterpart here. If you don't mind, I'd like to take him down to maintenance.

TROOPER: All right.

The guard nods and Threepio, with little Artoo in tow, hurries out the door.

INTERIOR: DEATH STAR—GARBAGE ROOM

As the walls rumble closed, the room gets smaller and smaller. Chewie is whining and trying to hold a wall back with his giant paws. Han is leaning back against the other wall. Garbage is snapping and popping. Luke is trying to reach Threepio.

LUKE: Threepio! Come in, Threepio! Threepio!

Han and Leia try to brace the contracting walls with a pole. Leia begins to sink into the trash.

HAN: Get to the top!

LEIA: I can't.

LUKE: Where could he be? Threepio! Threepio, will you come in?

INTERIOR: DEATH STAR—MAIN FORWARD BAY— SERVICE PANEL

THREEPIO: They aren't here! Something must have happened to them. See if they've been captured.

Little Artoo carefully plugs his claw arm into a new

wall socket and a complex array of electronic sounds spew from the tiny robot.

THREEPIO: Hurry!

INTERIOR: DEATH STAR—GARBAGE ROOM

The walls are only feet apart. Leia and Han are braced against the walls. The princess is frightened. They look at each other. Leia reaches out and takes Han's hand and holds it tightly. She's terrified and suddenly groans as she feels the first crushing pressure against her body.

HAN: One thing's for sure. We're all going to be a lot thinner! (to Leia) Get on top of it!

LEIA: I'm trying!

INTERIOR: DEATH STAR—MAIN FORWARD BAY— SERVICE PANEL

THREEPIO: (to Artoo) Thank goodness, they

haven't found them! Where could they be?

Artoo frantically beeps something to See-Threepio.

THREEPIO: Use the comlink? Oh, my! I forgot I turned it off!

INTERIOR: DEATH STAR—GARBAGE ROOM

Meanwhile, Luke is lying on his side, trying to keep his head above the rising ooze. Luke's comlink begins to buzz and he rips it off his belt.

INTERIOR: DEATH STAR—MAIN FORWARD BAY—SERVICE PANEL

Muffled sounds of Luke's voice over comlink can be heard, but not distinctly.

THREEPIO: Are you there, sir?

INTERIOR: DEATH STAR—GARBAGE ROOM

LUKE: Threepio!

INTERIOR: DEATH STAR—MAIN FORWARD BAY

THREEPIO: We've had some problems...

LUKE: (over comlink) Will you shut up and listen to me? Shut down all garbage mashers on the detention level, will you? Do you copy?

INTERIOR: DEATH STAR—GARBAGE ROOM

LUKE: Shut down all the garbage mashers on the detention level.

INTERIOR: DEATH STAR—MAIN FORWARD BAY—SERVICE PANEL

LUKE: (over comlink) Shut down all the garbage mashers on the detention level.

THREEPIO: (to Artoo) No. Shut them all down! Hurry!

Threepio holds his head in agony as he hears the incredible screaming and hollering from Luke's comlink.

THREEPIO: Listen to them! They're dying, Artoo! Curse my metal body! I wasn't fast enough. It's all my fault! My poor master!

LUKE: (over comlink) Threepio, we're all right!

INTERIOR: DEATH STAR—GARBAGE ROOM

The screaming and hollering is the sound of joyous relief. The walls have stopped moving. Han, Chewie and Leia embrace in the background.

LUKE: We're all right. You did great.

Luke moves to the pressure sensitive hatch, looking for a number.

LUKE: Hey... hey, open the pressure maintenance hatch on unit number... where are we?

INTERIOR: DEATH STAR—MAIN FORWARD BAY—SERVICE PANEL

Threepio looks at the computer panel as Han reads the number.

HAN: (over comlink) Three-two-six-eight-two-seven.

INTERIOR: DEATH STAR—TRACTOR BEAM—POWER GENERATOR TRENCH

Ben enters a humming service trench that powers the huge tractor beam. The trench seems to be a hundred

Above: Sketches of Death Star trench, Ralph McQuarrie

Right: Drawing of a stormtrooper,
Ralph McQuarrie

miles deep. The clacking sound of huge switching devices can be heard. The old Jedi edges his way along a narrow ledge leading to a control panel that connects two large cables. He carefully makes several adjustments in the computer terminal, and several lights on the board go from red to blue.

INTERIOR: DEATH STAR—UNUSED HALLWAY

The group exits the garbage room into a dusty, unused hallway. Han and Luke remove the trooper suits and strap on the blaster belts.

HAN: If we can just avoid any more female advice, we ought to be able to get out of here.

Luke smiles and scratches his head as he takes a blaster from Solo.

LUKE: Well, let's get moving!

Chewie begins growling and points to the hatch to the garbage room, as he runs away and then stops howling .

HAN: (to Chewie) Where are you going?

The Dia Nogu bangs against the hatch and a long, slimy tentacle works its way out of the doorway searching for a victim. Han aims his pistol.

LEIA: No, wait. They'll hear!

Han fires at the doorway. The noise of the blast echoes relentlessly throughout the empty passageway. Luke simply shakes his head in disgust.

HAN: (to Chewie) Come here, you big coward!

Chewie shakes his head "no."

Chewie! Come here!

LEIA: Listen. I don't know who you are, or where you come from, but from now on, you do as I tell you. Okay?

Han is stunned at the command of the petite young girl.

HAN: Look, Your Worshipfulness, let's get one thing straight! I take orders from one person! Me!

LEIA: It's a wonder you're still alive. (looking at Chewie) Will somebody get this big walking carpet out of my way?

Han watches her start away. He looks at Luke.

HAN: No reward is worth this.

They follow her, moving swiftly down the deserted corridor.

INTERIOR: DEATH STAR—POWER TRENCH

Suddenly a door behind Ben slides open and a detachment of stormtroopers marches to the power trench. Ben instantly slips into the shadows as an Officer moves to within a few feet of him.

OFFICER: Secure this entry area until the alert is cancelled.

FIRST TROOPER: Give me regular reports.

All but two of the stormtroopers leave.

FIRST TROOPER: Do you know what's going on?

SECOND TROOPER: Maybe it's another drill.

Ben moves around the tractor beam, watching the stormtroopers as they turn their backs to him. Ben gestures with his hand toward them, as the troops think they hear something in the other hallway. With the help of the Force, Ben deftly slips past the troopers and into the main hallway.

SECOND TROOPER: What was that?

FIRST TROOPER: Oh, it's nothing. Don't worry about it.

INTERIOR: DEATH STAR—HALLWAY

Luke, Han, Chewbacca, and Leia run down an empty hallway and stop before a bay window overlooking the pirateship. Troopers are milling around the ship. Luke takes out his pocket comlink.

HAN: (looking at his ship) There she is.

LUKE: See-Threepio, do you copy?

THREEPIO: (voice) For the moment. Uh, we're in the main hangar across from the ship.

LUKE: We're right above you. Stand by.

Han is watching the dozen or so troops moving in and out of the pirateship. Leia moves toward Han, touches his arm, and points out the window to the ship.

LEIA: You came in that thing? You're braver than I thought.

HAN: Nice! Come on!

Han gives her a dirty look, and they start off down the hallway. They round a corner and run right into twenty Imperial stormtroopers heading toward them. Both groups are taken by surprise and stop in their tracks.

FIRST TROOPER: It's them! Blast them!

Before even thinking, Han draws his laser pistol and charges the troops, firing. His blast knocks one of the stormtroopers into the air. Chewie follows his captain down the corridor, stepping over the fallen trooper on the floor.

HAN: (to Luke and Leia) Get back to the ship!

LUKE: Where are you going? Come back!

Han has already rounded a corner and does not hear.

LEIA: He certainly has courage.

LUKE: What good will it do us if he gets himself killed? Come on!

Luke is furious but doesn't have time to think about it for muted alarms begin to go off down on the hangar deck. Luke and Leia start off toward the starship hangar.

INTERIOR: DEATH STAR—SUBHALLWAY

Han chases the stormtroopers down a long subhallway. He is yelling and brandishing his laser pistol. The troops reach a dead end and are forced to turn and fight. Han stops a few feet from them and assumes a defensive position. The troops begin to raise their laser guns. Soon all ten troopers are moving into an attack position in front of the lone starpirate. Han's determined look begins to fade as the troops begin to advance. Solo jumps backward as they fire at him.

INTERIOR: DEATH STAR—SUBHALLWAY

Chewbacca runs down the subhallway in a last-ditch attempt to save his bold captain. Suddenly he hears the firing of laser guns and yelling. Around the corner shoots Han, pirate extraordinaire, running for his life, followed by a host of furious stormtroopers. Chewbacca turns and starts running the other way also.

INTERIOR: DEATH STAR—HALLWAY

Luke fires his laser pistol wildly as he and Leia rush down a narrow subhallway, chased by several stormtroopers. They quickly reach the end of the subhallway and race through an open hatchway.

INTERIOR: DEATH STAR—CENTRAL CORE SHAFT

Luke and Leia race through the hatch onto a narrow

Below: Sketch, John Mollo

bridge that spans a huge, deep shaft that seems to go into infinity. The bridge has been retracted into the wall of the shaft, and Luke almost rushes into the abyss. He loses his balance off the end of the bridge as Leia, behind him, takes hold of his arm and pulls him back.

LUKE: (gasping) I think we took a wrong turn.

Blasts from the stormtroopers' laser guns explode nearby reminding them of the oncoming danger. Luke fires back at the advancing troops. Leia reaches over and hits a switch that pops the hatch door shut with a resounding boom, leaving them precariously perched on a short piece of bridge overhang. Laserfire from the troopers continues to hit the steel door.

LEIA: There's no lock!

Luke blasts the controls with his laser pistol.

LUKE: That oughta hold it for a while.

LEIA: Quick, we've got to get across. Find the control that extends the bridge.

LUKE: Oh, I think I just blasted it.

Luke looks at the blasted bridge control while the stormtroopers on the oposite side of the door begin making ominous drilling and pounding sounds.

LEIA: They're coming through!

Luke notices something on his stormtrooper belt, when laserfire hits the wall behind him. Luke aims his laser pistol at a stormtrooper perched on a higher bridge overhang across the abyss from them. They exchange fire. Two more troopers appear on another overhang, also firing. A trooper is hit, and grabs at his chest.

Another trooper standing on a bridge overhang is hit by Luke's laserfire, and plummets down the shaft. Troopers move back off the bridge; Luke hands his gun to Leia.

LUKE: Here, hold this.

Luke pulls a thin nylon cable from his trooper utility belt. It has a grappler hook on it. A trooper appears on a bridge overhang and fires at Luke and Leia. As Luke works with the rope, Leia returns the laser volley. Another trooper appears and fires at them, as Leia returns his fire as well. Suddenly, the hatch door begins to open, revealing the feet of more troops.

LEIA: Here they come!

Leia hits one of the stormtroopers on the bridge above, and he falls into the abyss. Luke tosses the rope across the gorge and it wraps itself around an outcropping of pipes. He tugs on the rope to make sure it is secure, then grabs the princess in his arms. Leia looks at Luke, then kisses him quickly on the lips. Luke is very surprised.

LEIA: For luck!

Luke pushes off and they swing across the treacherous abyss to the corresponding hatchway on the opposite side. Just as Luke and Leia reach the far side of the canyon, the stormtroopers break through the hatch and begin to fire at the escaping duo. Luke returns the fire before ducking into the tiny subhallway.

INTERIOR: DEATH STAR—NARROW PASSAGEWAY

Ben hides in the shadows of a narrow passageway as several stormtroopers rush past him in the main hallway. He checks to make sure they're gone, then runs down the hallway in the opposite direction. Darth Vader appears at the far end of the hallway and starts after the old Jedi.

INTERIOR: DEATH STAR—MAIN FORWARD BAY

Threepio looks around at the troops milling about the pirateship entry ramp.

Facing page above and below: Costume sketches for Luke and Princess Leia, John Mollo; left: thumbnail sketch for swing across, Ralph McQuarrie; below: production painting, Ralph McQuarrie

THREEPIO: Where could they be?

Artoo, plugged into the computer socket, turns his dome left and right, beeping a response.

INTERIOR: DEATH STAR—CORRIDOR—BLAST SHIELD DOOR

Han and Chewbacca run down a long corridor with several troopers hot on their trail.
TROOPER: Close the blast doors!

At the end of the hallway, blast doors begin to close in front of them. The young starpilot and his furry companion race past the huge doors just as they are closing, and manage to get off a couple of laserblasts at the pursuing troops before the doors slam shut.
TROOPER: Open the blast doors! Open the blast doors!

INTERIOR: DEATH STAR—HALLWAY LEADING TO MAIN FORWARD BAY

Ben hurries along one of the tunnels leading to the hangar where the pirateship waits. Just before he reaches the hangar, Darth Vader steps into view at the end of the tunnel, not ten feet away. Vader lights his saber. Ben also ignites his and steps slowly forward.
VADER: I've been waiting for you, Obi-Wan. We meet again, at last. The circle is now complete.

Ben Kenobi moves with elegant ease into a classical offensive position. The fearsome Dark Knight takes a defensive stance.
VADER: When I left you, I was but the learner; now I am the master.
BEN: Only a master of evil, Darth.

The two Galactic warriors stand perfectly still for a few moments, sizing each other up and waiting for the right moment. Ben seems to be under increasing pressure and strain, as if an invisible weight were being placed upon him. He shakes his head and, blinking, tries to clear his eyes.

Ben makes a sudden lunge at the huge warrior but is

checked by a lightning movement of The Sith. A masterful slash stroke by Vader is blocked by the old Jedi. Another of the Jedi's blows is blocked, then countered. Ben moves around the Dark Lord and starts backing into the massive starship hangar. The two powerful warriors stand motionless for a few moments with laser swords locked in mid-air, creating a low buzzing sound.
VADER: Your powers are weak, old man.
BEN: You can't win, Darth. If you strike me down, I shall become more powerful than you can possibly imagine.

Their lightsabers continue to meet in combat.

INTERIOR: DEATH STAR—MAIN FORWARD BAY

Han Solo and Chewbacca, their weapons in hand, lean back against the wall surveying the forward bay, watching the Imperial stormtroopers make their rounds of the hangar.
HAN: Didn't we just leave this party?

Chewbacca growls a reply, as Luke and the princess join them.
HAN: What kept you?
LEIA: We ran into some old friends.
LUKE: Is the ship all right?
HAN: Seems okay, if we can get to it. Just hope the old man got the tractor beam out of commission.

INTERIOR: DEATH STAR—HALLWAY

Vader and Ben Kenobi continue their powerful duel. As they hit their lightsabers together, lightning flashes on impact. Troopers look on in interest as the old Jedi and Dark Lord of The Sith fight. Suddenly Luke spots the battle from his group's vantage point.
LUKE: Look!

Luke, Leia, Han and Chewie look up and see Ben and Vader emerging from the hallways on the far side of the docking bay.

INTERIOR: DEATH STAR—DOCKING BAY

Threepio and Artoo-Detoo are in the center of the Death Star's Imperial docking bay.
THREEPIO: Come on, Artoo, we're going!

Threepio ducks out of sight as the seven stormtroopers who were guarding the starship rush past them heading toward Ben and The Sith Knight. He pulls on Artoo.

INTERIOR: DEATH STAR—HALLWAY

Solo, Chewie, Luke, and Leia tensely watch the duel. The troops rush toward the battling knights.
HAN: Now's our chance! Go!

They start for the Millennium Falcon.
Ben sees the troops charging toward him and realizes

Storyboards, Ivor Beddoes

that he is trapped. Vader takes advantage of Ben's momentary distraction and brings his mighty lightsaber down on the old man. Ben manages to deflect the blow and swiftly turns around.

The old Jedi Knight looks over his shoulder at Luke, lifts his sword from Vader's, then watches his opponent with a serene look on his face.

Vader brings his sword down, cutting old Ben in half. Ben's cloak falls to the floor in two parts, but Ben is not in it. Vader is puzzled at Ben's disappearance and pokes at the empty cloak. As the guards are distracted, the adventurers and the robots reach the starship. Luke sees Ben cut in two and starts for him. Aghast, he yells out.

LUKE: No!

The stormtroopers turn toward Luke and begin firing at him. The robots are already moving up the ramp into the Millennium Falcon, while Luke, transfixed by anger and awe, returns their fire. Solo joins in the laserfire. Vader looks up and advances toward them, as one of his trooopers is struck down.

HAN: (to Luke) Come on!
LEIA: Come on! Luke, it's too late!
HAN: Blast the door! Kid!

Luke fires his laser pistol at the door control panel, and it explodes. The doors begin to slide shut. Three troopers charge forward firing laser bolts, as the door slides to a close behind them, shutting Vader and the other troops out of the docking bay. A stormtrooper lies dead at the feet of his onrushing compatriots. Luke starts for the advancing troops, as Solo and Leia move up the ramp into the pirateship. He fires, hitting a stormtrooper, who crumples to the floor.

BEN'S VOICE: Run, Luke! Run!

Luke looks around to see where the voice came from. He turns toward the pirateship, ducking Imperial gunfire from the troopers and races into the ship.

INTERIOR: MILLENNIUM FALCON—COCKPIT

Han pulls back on the controls and the ship begins to

move. The dull thud of laser bolts can be heard bouncing off the outside of the ship as Chewie adjusts his controls.
HAN: I hope the old man got that tractor beam out of commission, or this is going to be a real short trip. Okay, hit it!

Chewbacca growls in agreement.

EXTERIOR: MILLENNIUM FALCON

The Millennium Falcon powers away from the Death Star docking bay, makes a spectacular turn and disappears into the vastness of space.

INTERIOR: MILLENNIUM FALCON—CENTRAL HOLD AREA

Luke, saddened by the loss of Obi-Wan Kenobi, stares off blankly as the robots look on. Leia puts a blanket around him protectively, and Luke turns and looks up at her. She sits down beside him.

INTERIOR: MILLENNIUM FALCON—COCKPIT

Solo spots approaching enemy ships.
HAN: (to Chewie) We're coming up on their sentry ships. Hold 'em off! Angle the deflector shields while I charge up with the main guns!

INTERIOR: MILLENNIUM FALCON—CENTRAL HOLD AREA

Luke looks downward sadly, shaking his head back and forth, as the princess smiles comfortingly at him.
LUKE: I can't believe he's gone.
Artoo-Detoo beeps a reply.

Han Solo

LEIA: There wasn't anything you could have done.
   Han rushes into the hold area where Luke is sitting with the princess.
HAN: (to Luke) Come on, buddy, we're not out of this yet!

INTERIOR: MILLENNIUM
FALCON—GUNPORTS—COCKPIT

Solo climbs into his attack position in the topside gunport.

INTERIOR: MILLENNIUM FALCON—HOLD AREA

Luke gets up and moves out toward the gunports as Leia heads for the cockpit.

INTERIOR: MILLENNIUM
FALCON—GUNPORTS—COCKPIT

Luke climbs down the ladder into the gunport cockpit, settling into one of the two main laser cannons mounted in large rotating turrets on either side of the ship.

INTERIOR: MILLENNIUM FALCON—SOLO'S GUNPORT

Han adjusts his headset as he sits before the controls of his laser cannon, then speaks into the attached microphone.
HAN: (to Luke) You in, kid? Okay, stay sharp!

INTERIOR: MILLENNIUM
FALCON—GUNPORTS—COCKPIT

Chewbacca and Princess Leia search the heavens for the attacking TIE fighters. The Wookiee pulls back on the speed controls as the ship bounces slightly.

INTERIOR: MILLENNIUM FALCON– SOLO'S
GUNPORT—COCKPIT

Computer graphic readouts form on Solo's target screen, as Han reaches for controls.

INTERIOR: MILLENNIUM FALCON—GUNPORT—COCKPIT

Luke sits in readiness for the attack, his hand on the laser cannon's control button.

INTERIOR: MILLENNIUM FALCON—COCKPIT

Chewbacca spots the enemy ships and barks.
LEIA: (into intercom) Here they come!

INTERIOR: COCKPIT—POV (POINT OF VIEW) SPACE

The Imperial TIE fighters move toward the Millennium Falcon, one each veering off to the left and right of the pirateship.

INTERIOR: TIE FIGHTER—COCKPIT

The stars whip past behind the Imperial pilot as he adjusts his maneuvering joy stick.

EXTERIOR: MILLENNIUM FALCON—IN SPACE

The TIE fighter races past the Falcon, firing laser beams as it passes.

INTERIOR: MILLENNIUM FALCON—HOLD AREA

Threepio is seated in the hold area, next to Artoo-Detoo. The pirateship bounces and vibrates as the power goes out in the room and then comes back on.

INTERIOR: MILLENNIUM
FALCON—COCKPIT—GUNPORTS

A TIE fighter maneuvers in front of Han, who follows it and fires at it with the laser cannon. Luke does likewise, as the fighter streaks into view. The ship has suffered a minor hit, and bounces slightly.

EXTERIOR: SPACE

Two TIE fighters dive down toward the pirateship.

INTERIOR: MILLENNIUM FALCON—GUNPORTS

Luke fires at an unseen fighter.
LUKE: They're coming in too fast!

EXTERIOR: SPACE—MILLENNIUM FALCON/TIE FIGHTERS

Pan with pirateship as two TIE fighters charge through the background. Laserbolts streak from all the craft.

INTERIOR: MILLENNIUM FALCON
—CHEWBACCA

The ship shudders as a laserbolt hits very close to the cockpit. The Wookiee chatters something to Leia.

EXTERIOR: TIE FIGHTER—SPACE

Full shot of a TIE fighter as it moves fast through the frame, firing on the pirate starship.

EXTERIOR: SPACE—TIE FIGHTERS

The two TIE fighters fire a barrage of laserbeams at the pirateship.

INTERIOR: MILLENNIUM FALCON—MAIN PASSAGEWAY

A laser bolt streaks into the side of the pirateship. The ship lurches violently, throwing poor Threepio into a cabinet full of small computer chips.
THREEPIO: Oooh!

INTERIOR: MILLENNIUM FALCON—COCKPIT GUNPORTS

Leia watches the computer readouts as Chewbacca manipulates the ship's controls.
LEIA: We've lost lateral controls.
HAN: Don't worry, she'll hold together.
   An enemy laserbolt hits the pirateship's control panel, causing it to blow out in a shower of sparks.
HAN: (to ship) You hear me, baby? Hold together!
   Artoo-Detoo advances toward the smoking sparking control panel, dousing the inferno by spraying it with fire retardant beeping all the while.

INTERIOR: MILLENNIUM FALCON—GUNPORT

Luke swivels in his gun mount, following the TIE fighter with his laser cannon.

INTERIOR: MILLENNIUM FALCON—GUNPORT

Solo aims his laser cannon at the enemy fighters.

EXTERIOR: SPACE

A TIE fighter streaks in front of the starship.

INTERIOR: MILLENNIUM FALCON—COCKPIT

Leia watches the TIE ship fly over.

Opposite page and below:
Sketches of Han Solo,
Ralph McQuarrie

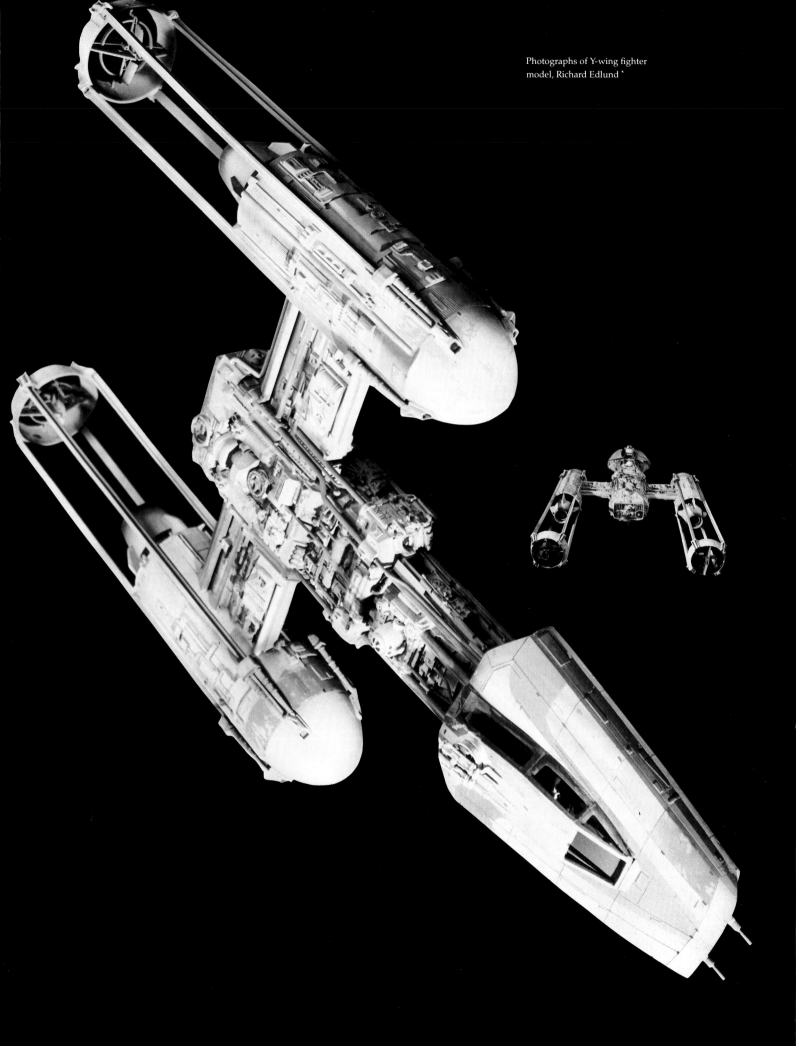

Photographs of Y-wing fighter
model, Richard Edlund `

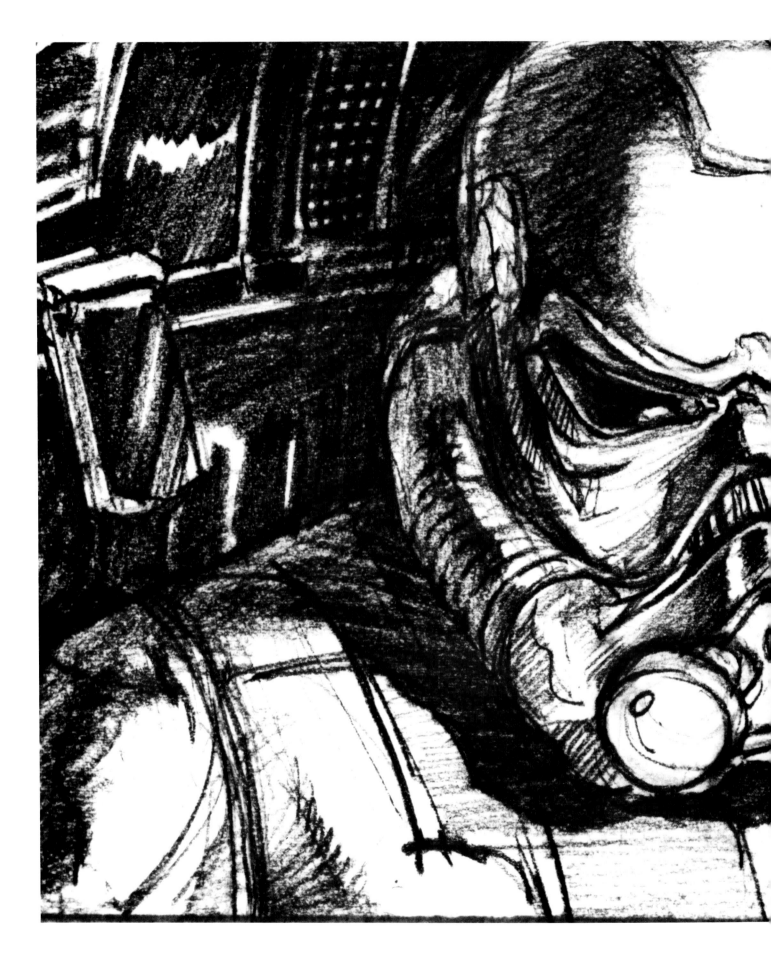

Storyboard, Alex Tavoularis

EXTERIOR: SPACE

A TIE fighter heads right for the pirateship, then zooms overhead.

INTERIOR: MILLENNIUM FALCON—GUNPORTS

Luke follows the TIE fighter across his field of view, firing laserbeams from his cannon.

EXTERIOR: TIE FIGHTER

A TIE fighter dives past the pirateship.

INTERIOR: MILLENNIUM FALCON—GUNPORTS

Luke fires at a TIE fighter. At his port, Han follows a fighter in his sights, releasing a blast of laserfire. He connects, and the fighter explodes into fiery dust. Han laughs victoriously.

EXTERIOR: SPACE

Two TIE fighters move toward and over the Millennium Falcon, unleashing a barrage of laserbolts at the ship.

INTERIOR: MILLENNIUM FALCON—GUNPORTS

Another TIE fighter moves in on the pirateship and Luke, smiling, fires the laser cannon at it, scoring a spectacular direct hit.
LUKE: Got him! I got him!
Han turns and gives Luke a victory wave which Luke gleefully returns.
HAN: Great kid! Don't get cocky.
Han turns back to his laser cannon.

EXTERIOR: SPACE

Two more TIE fighters cross in front of the pirateship.

INTERIOR: MILLENNIUM FALCON—COCKPIT

While Chewbacca manipulates the controls, Leia turns, looking over her shoulder out the ports.
LEIA: There are still two more of them out there!

EXTERIOR: SPACE

A TIE fighter moves up over the pirateship, firing laserblasts at it.

INTERIOR: MILLENNIUM FALCON—GUNPORTS

Luke and Han look into their respective projected target screens. An Imperial fighter crosses Solo's port, and Han swivels in his chair, following it with blasts from his laser cannon. Another fighter crosses Luke's port, and he reacts in a like manner, the glow of his target screen lighting his face.

EXTERIOR: SPACE

The TIE fighter zooms toward the pirateship, firing destructive blasts at it.

INTERIOR: MILLENNIUM FALCON—GUNPORTS

Luke fires a laserblast at the approaching enemy fighter, and it bursts into a spectacular explosion. Luke's projected screen gives a readout of the hit. The pirateship bounces slightly as it is struck by enemy fire.

EXTERIOR: SPACE—TIE FIGHTER

The last of the attacking Imperial TIE fighters looms in, firing upon the Falcon.

INTERIOR: MILLENNIUM FALCON—GUNPORT

Solo swivels behind his laser cannon, his aim describing the arc of the TIE fighter. The fighter comes closer, firing at the pirateship, but a well-aimed blast from Solo's laser cannon hits the attacker, which blows up in a small atomic shower of burning fragments.
LUKE: (laughing) That's it! We did it!
The princess jumps up and gives Chewie a congratulatory hug.
LEIA: We did it!

INTERIOR: MILLENNIUM FALCON—PASSAGEWAY

Threepio lies on the floor of the ship, completely tangled in the smoking, sparking wires.
THREEPIO Help! I think I'm melting! (to Artoo) This is all your fault.

Artoo turns his dome from side to side, beeping in response.

EXTERIOR: SPACE—MILLENNIUM FALCON

The victorious Millennium Falcon moves off majestically through space.

INTERIOR: DEATH STAR—CONTROL ROOM

Darth Vader strides into the control room, where Tarkin is watching the huge view screen. A sea of stars is before him.
TARKIN: Are they away?
VADER: They have just made the jump into hyperspace.
TARKIN: You're sure the homing beacon is secure aboard their ship? I'm taking an awful risk, Vader. This had better work.

INTERIOR: MILLENNIUM FALCON—COCKPIT

Han, removing his gloves and smiling, is at the controls of the ship. Chewie moves into the aft section to check the damage. Leia is seated near Han.
HAN: Not a bad bit of rescuing, huh? You know, sometimes I even amaze myself.
LEIA: That doesn't sound too hard. Besides, they let us go. It's the only explanation for the ease of our escape.
HAN: Easy... you call that easy?
LEIA: They're tracking us!
HAN: Not this ship, sister.
Frustrated, Leia shakes her head.
LEIA: At least the information in Artoo is still intact.
HAN: What's so important? What's he carrying?
LEIA: The technical readouts of that battle station. I only hope that when the data is analyzed, a weakness can be found. It's not over yet!
HAN: It is for me, sister! Look, I ain't in this for your revolution, and I'm not in it for you, Princess. I expect to be well paid. I'm in it for the money!
LEIA: You needn't worry about your reward. If money is all that you love, then that's what you'll receive!
She angrily turns, and as she starts out of the cockpit, passes Luke coming in.
LEIA: Your friend is quite a mercenary. I wonder if he really cares about anything... or anybody.
LUKE: I care!
Luke, shaking his head, sits in the copilot seat. He and Han stare out at the vast blackness of space.
LUKE: So... what do you think of her, Han?
HAN: I'm trying not to, kid!
LUKE: (under his breath) Good...
HAN: Still, she's got a lot of spirit. I don't know, what do you think? Do you think a princess and a guy like me...
LUKE: No!
Luke says it with finality and looks away. Han smiles at young Luke's jealousy.

EXTERIOR: SPACE AROUND FOURTH MOON OF YAVIN

The battered pirateship drifts into orbit around the planet Yavin and proceeds to one of its tiny green moons.

EXTERIOR: FOURTH MOON OF YAVIN

The pirateship soars over the dense jungle.

EXTERIOR: MASSASSI OUTPOST

An alert guard, his laser gun in hand, scans the countryside. He sets the gun down and looks toward the temple, barely visible in the foliage.

EXTERIOR: MASSASSI OUTPOST—JUNGLE TEMPLE

Rotting in a forest of gargantuan trees, an ancient temple lies shrouded in an eerie mist. The air is heavy with the fantastic cries of unimaginable creatures. Han, Luke and the others are greeted by the Rebel troops.
Luke and the group ride into the massive temple on an armored military speeder.

INTERIOR: MASSASSI—MAIN HANGAR DECK

The military speeder stops in a huge spaceship hangar, set up in the interior of the crumbling temple. Willard, the commander of the Rebel forces, rushes up to the group and gives Leia a big hug. Every one is pleased to see her.
WILLARD: (holding Leia) You're safe! We had feared the worst.
Willard composes himself, steps back and bows formally.
WILLARD: When we heard about Alderaan, we were afraid that you were... lost along with your father.
LEIA: We don't have time for our sorrows, Commander. The battle station has surely tracked us here (looking pointedly at Han). It's the only explanation for the ease of our escape. You must use the information in this R2 unit to plan the attack. It is our only hope.

EXTERIOR: SPACE

The surface of the Death Star ominously approaches the red planet Yavin.

INTERIOR: DEATH STAR—CONTROL ROOM

Grand Moff Tarkin and Lord Darth Vader are interrupted in their discussion by the buzz of the comlink. Tarkin moves to answer the call.

TARKIN: Yes.
DEATH STAR INTERCOM VOICE: We are approaching

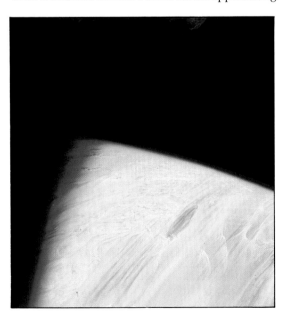

Opposite page and left: Matte paintings of Yavin, Ralph McQuarrie

Sketches and thumbnail for
production painting,
Ralph McQuarrie

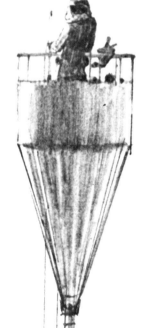

the planet Yavin. The Rebel base is on a moon on the far side. We are preparing to orbit the planet.

EXTERIOR: YAVIN—JUNGLE

A lone guard stands in a tower high above the Yavin landscape, surveying the countryside. A mist hangs over the jungle of twisted green.

INTERIOR: MASSASSI—WAR ROOM BRIEFING AREA

Dodonna stands before a large electronic wall display. Leia and several other senators are to one side of the giant readout. The low-ceilinged room is filled with starpilots, navigators, and a sprinkling of R2-type robots. Everyone is listening intently to what Dodonna is saying. Han and Chewbacca are standing near the back.

DODONNA: The battle station is heavily shielded and carries a firepower greater than half the star fleet. Its defenses are designed around a direct large-scale assault. A small one-man fighter should be able to penetrate the outer defense.

Gold Leader, a rough looking man in his early thirties, stands and addresses Dodonna.
GOLD LEADER: Pardon me for asking, sir, but what good are snub fighters going to be against that?
DODONNA: Well, the Empire doesn't consider a small one-man fighter to be any threat, or they'd have a tighter defense. An analysis of the plans provided by Princess Leia has demonstrated a weakness in the battle station.

Artoo-Detoo stands next to a similar robot, makes beeping sounds, and turns his head from right to left.

DODONNA: The approach will not be easy. You are required to maneuver straight down this trench and skim the surface to this point. The target area is only two meters wide. It's a small thermal exhaust port, right below the main port. The shaft leads directly to the reactor system. A precise hit will start a chain reaction which should destroy the station.

A murmer of disbelief runs through the room.

DODONNA: Only a precise hit will set up a chain reaction. The shaft is ray-shielded, so you'll have to use proton torpedoes.

Luke is sitting next to Wedge Antilles, a hotshot pilot about sixteen years old.

WEDGE: That's impossible, even for a computer.

LUKE: It's not impossible. I used to bull's-eye womp rats in my T-sixteen back home. They're not much bigger than two meters.

DODONNA: Man your ships! And may the Force be with you!

The group rises and begins to leave.

INTERIOR: SPACE

The Death Star begins to move around the planet toward the tiny green moon.

INTERIOR: DEATH STAR

Tarkin and Vader watch the computer projected screen with interest, as a circle of lights intertwines around one another on the screen showing its position in relation to Yavin and their fourth moon.

DEATH STAR INTERCOM VOICE: Orbiting the planet

at maximum velocity. The moon with the Rebel base will be in range in thirty minutes.

VADER: This will be a day long remembered. It has seen the end of Kenobi and will soon see the end of the Rebellion.

INTERIOR: MASSASSI OUTPOST—MAIN HANGAR DECK

Luke, Threepio and little Artoo enter the huge spaceship hangar and hurry along a long line of gleaming spacefighters. Flight crews rush around loading

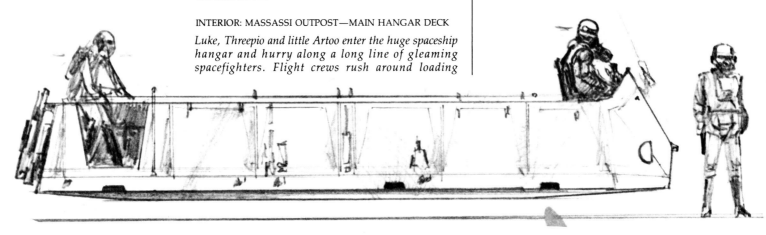

Sketches and production paintings, Ralph McQuarrie

last-minute armaments and unlocking power couplings. In an area isolated from this activity Luke finds Han and Chewbacca loading small boxes onto an armored speeder.

MAN'S VOICE: (over loudspeaker) All flight troops, man your stations. All flight troops, man your stations.

Han is deliberately ignoring the activity of the fighter pilots' preparations. Luke is quite saddened at the sight of his friend's departure.

LUKE: So... you got your reward and you're just leaving then?

HAN: That's right, yeah! I got some old debts I've got to pay off with this stuff. Even if I didn't, you don't think I'd be fool enough to stick around here, do you? Why don't you come with us? You're pretty good in a fight. I could use you.

LUKE: (getting angry) Come on! Why don't you take a look around? You know what's about to happen, what they're up against. They could use a good pilot like you. You're turning your back on them.

HAN: What good's a reward if you ain't around to use it? Besides, attacking that battle station ain't my idea of courage. It's more like suicide.

LUKE: All right. Well, take care of yourself, Han. I guess that's what you're best at, isn't it?

Luke goes off and Han hesitates, then calls to him.

HAN: Hey, Luke... may the Force be with you!

Luke turns and sees Han wink at him. Luke lifts his hand in a small wave and then goes off.

Han turns to Chewie who growls at his captain.

HAN: What're you lookin' at? I know what I'm doing.

INTERIOR: MAIN HANGAR DECK—LUKE'S SHIP

Luke, Leia, and Dodonna meet under a huge space fighter.

LEIA: What's wrong?

LUKE: Oh, it's Han! I don't know, I really thought he'd change his mind.

LEIA: He's got to follow his own path. No one can choose it for him.

LUKE: I only wish Ben were here.

Leia gives Luke a little kiss, turns, and goes off.

As Luke heads for his ship, another pilot rushes up to him and grabs his arm.

BIGGS: Luke! I don't believe it! How'd you get here... are you going out with us?!

LUKE: Biggs! Of course, I'll be up there with you! Listen, have I got some stories to tell you...

Red Leader, a rugged handsome man in his forties, comes up behind Luke and Biggs. He has the confident smile of a born leader.

RED LEADER: Are you... Luke Skywalker? Have you been checked out on the Incom T-sixty-five?

BIGGS: Sir, Luke is the best bushpilot in the outer rim territories.

Pilot Leader pats Luke on the back as they stop in front of his fighter.

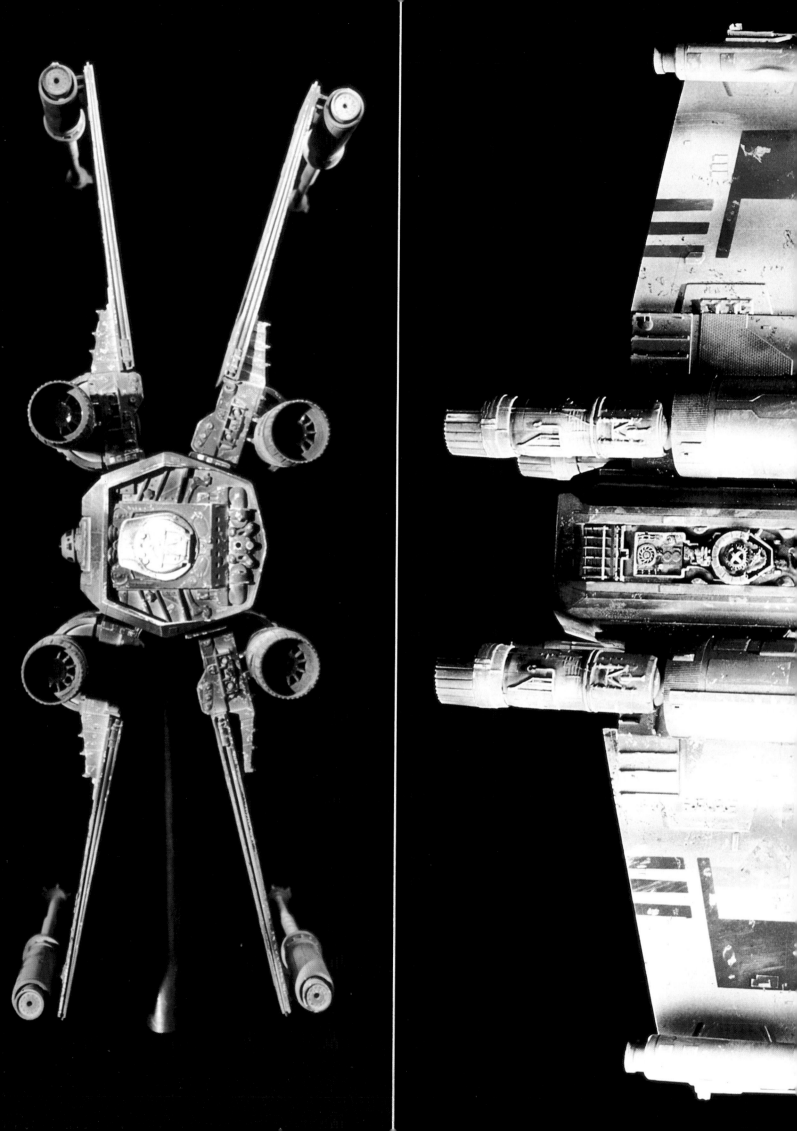

Photographs of X-Wing fighter
models, Richard Edlund

PILOT LEADER: I met your father once when I was just a boy, he was a great pilot. You'll do all right. If you've got half of your father's skill, you'll do better than all right.

LUKE: Thank you, sir. I'll try.

Red Leader hurries to his own ship.

BIGGS: I've got to get aboard. Listen, you'll tell me your stories when we come back. All right?

LUKE: I told you I'd make it someday, Biggs.

BIGGS: (going off) You did, all right. It's going to be like old times Luke. We're a couple of shooting stars that'll never be stopped!

Luke laughs and shakes his head in agreement. He heads for his ship.

As Luke begins to climb up the ladder into his sleek, deadly spaceship, the crew chief, who is working on the craft, points to little Artoo, who is being hoisted into a socket on the back of the fighter.

CHIEF: This R2 unit of yours seems a bit beat up. Do you want a new one?

LUKE: Not on your life! That little droid and I have been through a lot together. (to Artoo) You okay, Artoo?

The crewmen lower Artoo-Detoo into the craft. Now a part of the exterior shell of the starship, the little droid beeps that he is fine.

Luke climbs up into the cockpit of his fighter and puts on his helmet. Threepio looks on from the floor of the massive hangar as the crewmen secure his little electronic partner into Luke's X-wing. It's an emotion-filled moment as Artoo beeps good-by.

CHIEF: Okay, easy she goes!

THREEPIO: Hang on tight, Artoo, you've got to come back.

Artoo beeps in agreement.

THREEPIO: You wouldn't want my life to get boring, would you?

Artoo whistles his reply.

All final preparations are made for the approaching battle. The hangar is buzzing with the last minute activity as the pilots and crewmen alike make their final adjustments. The hum of activity is occasionally trespassed by the distorted voice of the loudspeaker issuing commands. Coupling hoses are disconnected from the ships as they are fueled. Cockpit shields roll smoothly into place over each pilot. A signalman, holding red

guiding lights, directs the ships. Luke, a trace of a smile gracing his lips, peers about through his goggles.

BEN'S VOICE: Luke, the Force will be with you.

Luke is confused at the voice and taps his headphones.

EXTERIOR: MASSASSI OUTPOST—JUNGLE

All that can be seen of the fortress is a lone guard standing on a small pedestal jutting out above the dense jungle. The muted gruesome crying sounds that naturally permeate this eerie purgatory are overwhelmed by the thundering din of ion rockets as four silver starships catapult from the foliage in a tight formation and disappear into the morning cloud cover.

INTERIOR: MASSASSI OUTPOST—WAR ROOM

The princess, Threepio, and a field commander sit quietly before the giant display showing the planet Yavin and its four moons. The red dot that represents the Death Star moves ever closer to the system. A series of green dots appear around the fourth moon. A din of indistinct chatter fills the war room.

MASSASSI INTERCOM VOICE: Stand-by alert. Death Star approaching. Estimated time to firing range, fifteen minutes.

Above: Sketches of Rebel
hideout, Ralph McQuarrie,
Left: Transport vehicle,
Ralph McQuarrie

Opposite page: Production
paintings, Ralph McQuarrie;

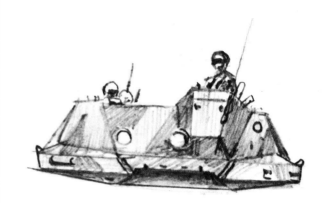

EXTERIOR: SPACE

The Death Star slowly moves behind the massive yellow surface of Yavin in the foreground, as many X-wing fighters flying in formation zoom toward us and out of the frame.

EXTERIOR: SPACE—ANOTHER ANGLE

Light from a distant sun creates an eerie atmospheric glow around a huge planet, Yavin. Rebel fighters flying in formation settle ominously in the foreground and very slowly pull away.

INTERIOR: RED LEADER STARSHIP—COCKPIT

Red Leader lowers his visor and adjusts his gun sights, looking to each side at his wing men.
RED LEADER: All Wings report in.

INTERIOR: ANOTHER COCKPIT

One of the Rebel fighters checks in through his mike.
RED TEN: Red Ten standing by.

INTERIOR: BIGGS'S COCKPIT

Biggs checks his fighter's controls, alert and ready for combat.
RED SEVEN: (over Bigg's headset) Red Seven standing by.
BIGGS: Red Three standing by.

INTERIOR: PORKINS' COCKPIT

PORKINS: Red Six standing by.
RED NINE: (over headset) Red Nine standing by.

INTERIOR: WEDGE'S FIGHTER—COCKPIT

WEDGE: Red Two standing by.

INTERIOR: LUKE'S X-WING FIGHTER—COCKPIT

RED ELEVEN: (over headset) Red Eleven standing by.
LUKE: Red Five standing by.

EXTERIOR: LUKE'S X-WING FIGHTER

Artoo-Detoo, in position outside of the fighter, turns his head from side to side and makes beeping sounds.

INTERIOR: RED LEADER'S FIGHTER—COCKPIT

RED LEADER: Lock S-foils in attack position.

EXTERIOR: SPACE

The group of X-wing fighters move in formation toward the Death Star, unfolding the wings and locking them into the "X" position.

INTERIOR: BIGGS'S COCKPIT

RED LEADER: (over headset) We're passing through their magnetic field.

INTERIOR: RED LEADER'S COCKPIT

RED LEADER: Hold tight!

INTERIOR: LUKE'S X-WING FIGHTER—COCKPIT

Luke adjusts his controls as he concentrates on the approaching Death Star. The ship begins to be buffeted slightly.
RED LEADER: (over headset) Switch your deflectors on.

INTERIOR: ANOTHER COCKPIT

RED LEADER: (over headset) Double front!

EXTERIOR: SPACE

The fighters, now X-shaped darts, move in formation. The Death Star now appears to be a small moon growing rapidly in size as the Rebel fighters approach. Complex patterns on the metallic surface begin to become visible. A large dish antenna is built into the surface on one side.

INTERIOR: WEDGE'S COCKPIT

Wedge is amazed and slightly frightened at the awesome spectacle.
WEDGE: Look at the size of that thing!
RED LEADER: (over headset) Cut the chatter, Red Two.

INTERIOR: RED LEADER'S COCKPIT

RED LEADER: Accelerate to attack speed. This is it, boys!

EXTERIOR: SPACE

As the fighters move closer to the Death Star, the awesome size of the gargantuan Imperial fortress is revealed. Half of the deadly space station is in shadow and this area sparkles with thousands of small lights running in thin lines and occasionally grouped in large clusters; somewhat like a city at night as seen from a weather satellite.

INTERIOR: GOLD LEADER'S COCKPIT

GOLD LEADER: Red Leader, this is Gold Leader.
RED LEADER: (over headset) I copy, Gold Leader.
GOLD LEADER: We're starting for the target shaft now.

INTERIOR: RED LEADER'S COCKPIT

Red Leader looks around at his wingmen; the Death Star looming in from behind. Two Y-wing fighters bob back and forth in the background. He moves his computer targeting device into position.

RED LEADER: We're in position. I'm going to cut across the axis and try and draw their fire.

EXTERIOR: SPACE

Two squads of Rebel fighters peel off. The X-wings dive toward the Death Star surface. A thousand lights glow across the dark grey expanse of the huge station.

INTERIOR: DEATH STAR

Alarm sirens scream as soldiers scramble to large turbo-powered laser gun emplacements. Electronic drivers rotate the huge guns into position as the crew adjusts their targeting devices.

EXTERIOR: SPACE AROUND THE DEATH STAR

Opposite page: Composite photo-graph; models photographed by Richard Edlund, airbrushing, Ralph McQuarrie

Above and below: Sketches of Rebels, Ralph McQuarrie

Costume sketches of Rebels and
Stormtroopers, Ralph McQuarrie

Laserbolts streak through the star-filled night. The Rebel X-wing fighters move in toward the Imperial base, as the Death Star aims its massive laser guns at the Rebel forces and fires.

INTERIOR: MASSASSI OUTPOST—WAR ROOM

Princess Leia listens to the battle over the intercom. Threepio is at her side.
WEDGE: (over war room speaker system) Heavy fire, boss! Twenty-three degrees.
RED LEADER: (over speaker) I see it. Stay low.

EXTERIOR: SPACE

An X-wing zooms across the surface of the Death Star.

INTERIOR: DEATH STAR

Technical crews scurry here and there loading last-minute armaments and unlocking power cables.

INTERIOR: WEDGE'S COCKPIT

Wedge maneuvers his fighter toward the menacing Death Star.

EXTERIOR: SPACE

X-wings continue in their attack course on the Death Star.

INTERIOR: LUKE'S X-WING FIGHTER—COCKPIT

Luke nosedives radically, starting his attack on the monstrous fortress. The Death Star surface streaks past the cockpit window.
LUKE: This is Red Five; I'm going in!

EXTERIOR: SPACE

Luke's X-wing races toward the Death Star. Laserbolts streak from Luke's weapons, creating a huge fireball explosion on the dim surface.

INTERIOR: LUKE'S X-WING FIGHTER—COCKPIT

Terror crosses Luke's face as he realizes he won't be able to pull out in time to avoid the fireball.
BIGGS: (over headset) Luke, pull out!

EXTERIOR: SURFACE OF DEATH STAR

Below and right: Sketches, Ralph McQuarrie

Luke's ship emerges from the fireball, with the leading edges of his wings slightly scorched.

INTERIOR: BIGGS'S COCKPIT

BIGGS: Are you all right?

INTERIOR: LUKE'S X-WING FIGHTER—COCKPIT

Luke adjusts his controls and breathes a sigh of relief. Flak bursts outside the cockpit window.
LUKE: I got a little cooked, but I'm okay.

EXTERIOR: SURFACE OF THE DEATH STAR

Rebel fighters continue to strafe the Death Star's surface with laserbolts.

INTERIOR: DEATH STAR

Walls buckle and cave in. Troops and equipment are blown in all directions. Stormtroopers stagger out of the rubble. Standing in the middle of the chaos, a vision of calm and foreboding, is Darth Vader. One of his Astro-Officers rushes up to him.
ASTRO–OFFICER: We count thirty Rebel ships, Lord Vader. But they're so small they're evading our turbo-lasers!
VADER: We'll have to destroy them ship to ship. Get the crews to their fighters.

INTERIOR: DEATH STAR

Smoke belches from the giant laser guns as they wind up their turbine generators to create sufficient power. The crew rushes about preparing for another blast. Even the troopers head gear is not adequate to protect them from the overwhelming noise of the monstrous weapon. One trooper bangs his helmet with his hand in an attempt to stop the ringing.

INTERIOR: RED LEADER'S X-WING—COCKPIT—TRAVELING

Red Leader flies through a heavy hail of flak.
RED LEADER: Luke, let me know when you're going in.

INTERIOR: LUKE'S X-WING—COCKPIT—TRAVELING

The Red Leader's X-wing flies past Luke as he puts his nose down and starts his attack dive.
LUKE: I'm on my way in now...
RED LEADER: Watch yourself! There's a lot of fire coming from the right side of that deflection tower.
LUKE: I'm on it.

EXTERIOR: SURFACE OF THE DEATH STAR

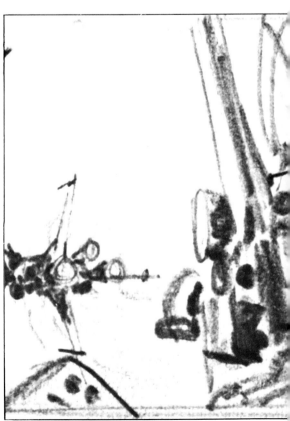

Luke flings his X-wing into a twisting dive across the horizons and down onto the dim grey surface.

EXTERIOR: LUKE'S X-WING—TRAVELING

A shot hurls from Luke's guns. Laserbolts streak toward the onrushing Death Star surface. Several small radar emplacements erupt in flame. Laserfire erupts from a protruding tower on the surface.

INTERIOR: LUKE'S X-WING—COCKPIT—TRAVELING

The blurry Death Star surface races past the cockpit window as a big smile sweeps across Luke's face at the success of his run. Flak thunders on all sides of him.

EXTERIOR: SURFACE OF THE DEATH STAR

The Death Star superstructure races past Luke as he maneuvers his craft through a wall of laserfire and peels away from the surface towards the heavens.

INTERIOR: DEATH STAR

The thunder and smoke of the big guns reverberate throughout the massive structure. Many soldiers rush about in the smoke and chaos, silhouetted by the almost continual flash of explosions.

INTERIOR: BIGGS'S COCKPIT—TRAVELING

Biggs dives through a forest of radar domes, antennae, and gun towers as he shoots low across the Death Star surface. A dense barrage of laserfire streaks by on all sides.

INTERIOR: DEATH STAR

Imperial star pilots dash in unison to a line of small auxiliary hatches that lead to Imperial TIE fighters.

INTERIOR: MASSASSI OUTPOST—WAR ROOM

Princess Leia, surrounded by her generals and aides, paces nervously before a lighted computer table. On all sides technicians work in front of many lighted glass walls. Dodonna watches quietly from one corner. One of the officers working over a screen speaks into his headset.
CONTROL OFFICER: Squad leaders, we've picked up a new group of signals. Enemy fighters coming your way.

INTERIOR: LUKE'S X-WING FIGHTER—COCKPIT—TRAVELING

Luke looks around to see if he can spot the approaching Imperial fighter.
LUKE: My scope's negative. I don't see anything.

INTERIOR: RED LEADER'S X-WING—COCKPIT—TRAVELING

The Death Star's surface sweeps past as Red Leader searches the sky for the Imperial fighter. Flak pounds at this ship.

RED LEADER: Keep up your visual scanning. With all this jamming, they'll be on top of you before your scope can pick them up.

EXTERIOR: SURFACE OF THE DEATH STAR

Silhouetted against the rim lights of the Death Star horizon, four ferocious Imperial TIE ships dive on the Rebel fighters. Two of the TIE fighters peel off and drop out of frame. Pan with the remaining two TIE ships.

INTERIOR: BIGGS'S COCKPIT—TRAVELING

Biggs panics when he discovers a TIE ship on his tail. The

Below: Sketch, Joe Johnston

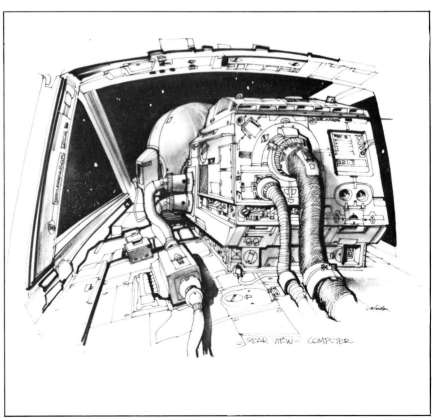

Production painting, Ralph McQuarrie

horizon in the background twists around as he peels off, hoping to lose the Imperial fighter.

INTERIOR: RED LEADER'S COCKPIT

RED LEADER: Biggs! You've picked one up...watch it!
BIGGS: I can't see it! Where is he?!

EXTERIOR: SPACE AROUND THE DEATH STAR

Biggs zooms off the surface and into space, closely followed by an Imperial TIE fighter. The TIE ship fires several laserbolts at Biggs, but misses.

INTERIOR: BIGGS'S COCKPIT—TRAVELING

Biggs sees the TIE ship behind him and swings around, trying to avoid him.
BIGGS: He's on me tight, I can't shake him...I can't shake him.

EXTERIOR: SPACE AROUND THE DEATH STAR

Biggs, flying at high altitude, peels off and dives toward the Death Star surface, but he is unable to lose the TIE fighter, who sticks close to his tail.

INTERIOR: X-WING FIGHTER—COCKPIT—TRAVELING

Luke is flying upside down. He rotates his ship around to a normal attitude as he comes out of his dive.
LUKE: Hang on, Biggs, I'm coming in.

EXTERIOR: SPACE AROUND THE DEATH STAR

Biggs and the tailing TIE ship dive for the surface, now followed by a fast-gaining Luke. After Biggs dives out of sight, Luke chases the Imperial fighter.

EXTERIOR: SURFACE OF THE DEATH STAR

In the foreground, the Imperial fighter races across the Death Star's surface, closely followed by Luke in the background.

INTERIOR: LUKE'S X-WING
FIGHTER—COCKPIT—TRAVELING

There is a shot from Luke's X-wing of the TIE ship exploding in a mass of flames.
LUKE: Got him!

INTERIOR: DEATH STAR

Darth Vader strides purposefully down a Death Star corridor, flanked by Imperial stormtroopers.
VADER: Several fighters have broken off from the main group. Come with me!

INTERIOR: MASSASSI OUTPOST—WAR ROOM

A concerned Princess Leia, Threepio, Dodonna, and other officers of the Rebellion stand around the huge round readout screen, listening to the ship-to-ship communication on the room's loudspeaker.
BIGGS: (over speaker) Pull in! Luke...pull in!
WEDGE: (over speaker) Watch your back, Luke!

INTERIOR: LUKE'S X-WING FIGHTER—COCKPIT

WEDGE (over headset) Watch your back! Fighter's above you, coming in!

EXTERIOR: SPACE

Luke's ship soars away from the Death Star's surface as he spots the tailing TIE fighter.

INTERIOR: TIE FIGHTER'S COCKPIT

The TIE pilot takes aim at Luke's X-wing.

EXTERIOR: SPACE

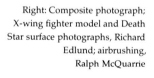
Right: Composite photograph; X-wing fighter model and Death Star surface photographs, Richard Edlund; airbrushing, Ralph McQuarrie

The Imperial TIE fighter pilot scores a hit on Luke's ship. Fire breaks out on the right side of the X-wing.

INTERIOR: LUKE'S X-WING FIGHTER—COCKPIT

Luke looks out of his cockpit at the flames on his ship.
LUKE: I'm hit, but not bad.

EXTERIOR: LUKE'S X-WING FIGHTER

Smoke pours out from behind Artoo-Detoo.
LUKE'S VOICE: Artoo, see what you can do with it. Hang on back there.
Green laserfire moves past the beeping little robot as his head turns.

INTERIOR: LUKE'S X-WING—COCKPIT

Luke nervously works his controls.
RED LEADER: (over headset) Red Six...

INTERIOR: MASSASSI OUTPOST—WAR ROOM

In the war room, Leia stands frozen as she listens and worries about Luke.
RED LEADER: (over speaker) Can you see Red Five?
RED TEN: (over speaker) There's a heavy fire zone on this side. Red Five, where are you?

INTERIOR: LUKE'S X-WING—COCKPIT

Luke spots the TIE fighters behind him and soars away from the Death Star surface.
LUKE: I can't shake him!

EXTERIOR: SURFACE OF THE DEATH STAR

Luke's ship soars closer to the surface of the Death Star, an Imperial TIE fighter closing in on him in hot pursuit.

INTERIOR: WEDGE'S COCKPIT

The Death Star whips below Wedge.
WEDGE: I'm on him, Luke!

INTERIOR: LUKE'S X-WING—COCKPIT

WEDGE: (over headset) Hold on!

EXTERIOR: SURFACE OF THE DEATH STAR

Wedge dives across the horizon toward Luke and the TIE fighter.

INTERIOR: WEDGE'S COCKPIT

Wedge moves his X-wing in rapidly.

INTERIOR: LUKE'S X-WING—COCKPIT

Luke reacts frantically.
LUKE: Blast it! Wedge, where are you?

INTERIOR: TIE FIGHTER—COCKPIT

The fighter pilot watches Wedge's X-wing approach. Another X-wing joins him, and both unleash a volley of laserfire on the Imperial fighter.

EXTERIOR: SPACE

The TIE fighter explodes, filling the screen with white light. Luke's ship can be seen far in the distance.

INTERIOR: LUKE'S X-WING—COCKPIT

Luke looks about in relief.
LUKE: Thanks, Wedge.

INTERIOR: MASSASSI OUTPOST—WAR ROOM

Leia, Threepio, Dodonna and other Rebel officers are listening to the Rebel Fighter's radio transmissions over the war room intercom.
BIGGS: (over speaker) Good shooting, Wedge!
GOLD LEADER: (over speaker) Red Leader...

INTERIOR: GOLD LEADER'S Y-WING—COCKPIT

Gold Leader peels off and starts toward the long trenches at the Death Star surface pole.
GOLD LEADER: ...This is Gold Leader. We're starting our attack run.

EXTERIOR: SPACE AROUND THE DEATH STAR

Three Y-wing fighters of the Gold group dive out of the stars toward the Death Star surface.

INTERIOR: MASSASSI OUTPOST—WAR ROOM

Leia and the others are grouped around the screen, as technicians move about attending to their duties.
RED LEADER: (over speaker) I copy, Gold Leader. Move into position.

EXTERIOR: SPACE AROUND THE DEATH STAR

Three Imperial TIE ships in precise formation dive toward the Death Star surface.

INTERIOR: DARTH VADER'S COCKPIT

Darth Vader calmly adjusts his control stick as the stars whip past in the window above his head.
VADER: Stay in attack formation!

Below: Rebel pilot helmet, John Mollo

INTERIOR: MASSASSI OUTPOST—WAR ROOM

Technicians are seated at the computer readout table.
GOLD LEADER: (over speaker) The exhaust port is...

INTERIOR: GOLD LEADER'S Y-WING—COCKPIT
GOLD LEADER: ...marked and locked in!

EXTERIOR: SPACE AROUND THE DEATH STAR

Gold Leader approaches the surface and pulls out to skim the surface of the huge station. The ship moves into a deep trench, firing laserbolts. The surface streaks past as laserfire is returned by the Death Star.

INTERIOR: GOLD FIVE'S Y-WING—COCKPIT—TRAVELING

Gold Five is a pilot in his early fifties with a very battered helmet that looks like it's been through many battles. He looks around to see if enemy ships are near. His fighter is buffeted by Imperial flak.

Above: Darth Vader costume
sketch, Ralph McQuarrie;
below: storyboards,
Gary Myers, Paul Huston, Steve
Gawley, Ronnie Shepherd; under
direction of Joe Johnston

INTERIOR: GOLD LEADER'S Y-WING—COCKPIT

Gold Leader races down the enormous trench that leads to

the exhaust port. Laserbolts blast toward him in increasing numbers, occasionally exploding near the ship causing it to bounce about.
GOLD LEADER: Switch power to front deflector screens.

EXTERIOR: SURFACE OF THE DEATH STAR

Three Y-wings skim the Death Star surface deep in the trench, as laserbolts streak past on all sides.

EXTERIOR: DEATH STAR SURFACE—GUN EMPLACEMENT

An exterior surface gun blazes away at the oncoming Rebel fighters.

INTERIOR: GOLD LEADER'S Y-WING—COCKPIT

GOLD LEADER: How many guns do you think, Gold Five?

INTERIOR: MASSASSI OUTPOST—WAR ROOM

GOLD FIVE: (over speaker) I'd say about twenty guns. Some on the surface, some on the towers.
Leia, Threepio, and the technicians view the projected target screen, as red and blue target lights glow. The red target near the center blinks on and off.
MASSASSI INTERCOM VOICE: (over speaker) Death Star will be in range in five minutes.

EXTERIOR: SURFACE OF THE DEATH STAR

The three Y-wing fighters race toward camera and zoom overhead through a hail of laserfire.

INTERIOR: GOLD LEADER'S Y-WING—COCKPIT

Gold Leader pulls his computer targeting device down in front of his eye. Laserbolts continue to batter the Rebel craft.
GOLD LEADER: Switch to targeting computer.

INTERIOR: GOLD TWO'S Y-WING—COCKPIT

Gold Two, a younger pilot about Luke's age, pulls down his targeting eye viewer and adjusts it. His ship shudders under intense laser barrage.
GOLD TWO: Computer's locked. Getting a signal.
As the fighters begin to approach the target area, suddenly all the laserfire stops. An eerie calm clings over the trench as the surface whips past in a blur.
GOLD TWO: The guns...they've stopped!

EXTERIOR: SURFACE OF THE DEATH STAR

Two Y-wings zoom down the Death Star trench.

INTERIOR: GOLD FIVE'S COCKPIT

Gold Five looks behind him.
GOLD FIVE: Stabilize your rear deflectors. Watch for enemy fighters.

INTERIOR: GOLD LEADER'S Y-WING—COCKPIT

GOLD LEADER: They're coming in! Three marks at two ten.

EXTERIOR: SPACE AROUND THE DEATH STAR

Three Imperial TIE ships, Darth Vader in the center flanked by two wingmen, dive in precise formation almost vertically toward the Death Star surface.

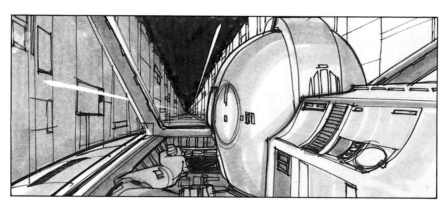

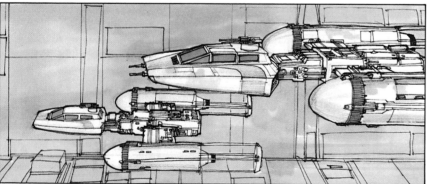

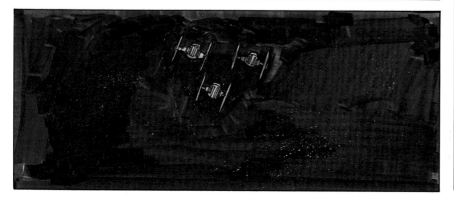

INTERIOR: DARTH VADER'S COCKPIT

Darth Vader calmly adjusts his control stick as the stars zoom by.
VADER: I'll take them myself! Cover me!
WINGMAN'S VOICE: (over speaker) Yes, sir.

EXTERIOR: SPACE AROUND THE DEATH STAR SURFACE

Three TIE fighters zoom across the surface of the Death

INTERIOR: DARTH VADER'S COCKPIT

Vader lines up Gold Two in his targeting computer. Vader's hands grip the control stick as he presses the button.

INTERIOR: GOLD TWO'S Y-WING—COCKPIT

The cockpit explodes around Gold Two. His head falls forward.

EXTERIOR: SPACE AROUND THE DEATH STAR

As Gold Two's ship explodes, debris is flung out into space.

INTERIOR: GOLD LEADER'S Y-WING—COCKPIT

Gold Leader looks over his shoulder at the scene.

INTERIOR: DEATH STAR TRENCH

The three TIE fighters race along in the trench in a tight formation.

INTERIOR: GOLD LEADER'S Y-WING—COCKPIT

Gold Leader panics.
GOLD LEADER: (into mike) I can't maneuver!

INTERIOR: GOLD FIVE'S Y-WING—COCKPIT

Gold Five, the old veteran, trys to calm Gold Leader.
GOLD FIVE: Stay on target.

INTERIOR: GOLD LEADER'S Y-WING—COCKPIT

The Death Star races by outside the cockpit window as he adjusts his targeting device.
GOLD LEADER: We're too close.

INTERIOR: GOLD FIVE'S Y-WING—COCKPIT

The older pilot remains calm.
GOLD FIVE: Stay on target!

INTERIOR: GOLD LEADER'S Y-WING—COCKPIT

Now he's really panicked.
GOLD LEADER: Loosen up!

INTERIOR: DARTH VADER'S COCKPIT

Vader calmly adjusts his targeting computer and pushes the fire button.

INTERIOR: GOLD LEADER'S Y-WING—COCKPIT

Gold Leader's ship is hit by Vader's lasers.

EXTERIOR: SURFACE OF THE DEATH STAR

Gold Leader explodes in a ball of flames, throwing debris

in all directions.

INTERIOR: GOLD FIVE'S Y-WING—COCKPIT

Gold Five moves in on the exhaust port.
GOLD FIVE: Gold Five to Red Leader...

INTERIOR: LUKE'S X-WING FIGHTER—COCKPIT

Luke looks over his shoulder at the action outside of his cockpit.
GOLD FIVE: (over headset) Lost Tiree, lost Dutch.

INTERIOR: RED LEADER'S COCKPIT

RED LEADER: I copy, Gold five.

INTERIOR: GOLD FIVE'S Y-WING—COCKPIT

GOLD FIVE: They came from behind....

EXTERIOR: SURFACE OF THE DEATH STAR

One of the engines explodes on Gold Five's Y-wing fighter, blazing out of control. He dives past the horizon

Above: Darth Vader costume sketch, Ralph McQuarrie; below: storyboards, Gary Myers, Paul Huston, Steve Gawley, Ronnie Shepherd; under direction of Joe Johnston

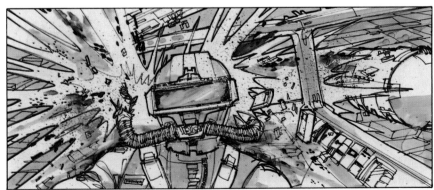

toward the Death Star's surface, passing a TIE fighter during his descent. Gold Five, a veteran of countless campaigns, spins toward his death.

INTERIOR: LUKE'S X-WING FIGHTER—COCKPIT

Luke looks nervously about him at the explosive battle.

INTERIOR: DEATH STAR—CONTROL ROOM

Grand Moff Tarkin and a Chief Officer stand in the Death Star's control room.
OFFICER: We've analyzed their attack, sir, and there is a danger. Should I have your ship standing by?
TARKIN: Evacuate? In our moment of triumph? I think you overestimate their chances!
   Tarkin turns to the computer readout screen. Flames

move around the green disk at the center of the screen, as numbers read across the bottom.
VOICE: (over speaker) Rebel base, three minutes and closing.

INTERIOR: RED LEADER'S COCKPIT

Red Leader looks over at his wingmen.
RED LEADER: Red Group, this is Red Leader.

INTERIOR: MASSASSI OUTPOST—WAR ROOM

Dodonna moves to the intercom as he fiddles with the computer keys.
RED LEADER: (over speaker) Rendezvous at mark six point one.
WEDGE: (over speaker) This is Red Two. Flying towards you.

Right: Sketch of Death Star Tower, Joe Johnston

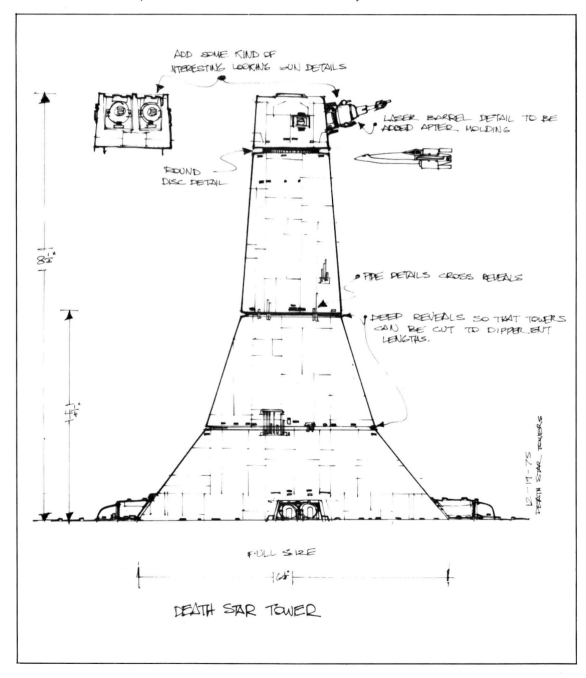

BIGGS: (over speaker) Red Three, standing by.

INTERIOR: RED LEADER'S COCKPIT

DODONNA: (over headset) Red Leader, this is Base One. Keep half your group out of range for the next run.

INTERIOR: LUKE'S X-WING FIGHTER—COCKPIT

RED LEADER'S VOICE: (over headset) Copy, Base One. Luke, take Red Two and Three. Hold up here and wait for my signal...to start your run.
Luke nods his head.

EXTERIOR: SPACE AROUND THE DEATH STAR

The X-wing fighters of Luke, Biggs, and Wedge fly in formation high above the Death Star's surface.

INTERIOR: LUKE'S X-WING FIGHTER—COCKPIT

Luke peers out from his cockpit.

EXTERIOR: SURFACE OF THE DEATH STAR

Two X-wings move across the surface of the Death Star. Red Leader's X-wing drops down to the surface leading to the exhaust port.

INTERIOR: RED LEADER'S COCKPIT

Red Leader looks around to watch for the TIE fighters. He begins to perspire.
RED LEADER: This is it!

EXTERIOR: SPACE

Red Leader roams down the trench of the Death Star as lasers streak across the black heavens.

EXTERIOR: DEATH STAR SURFACE—GUN EMPLACEMENT

A huge remote-control laser cannon fires at the approaching Rebel fighters.

EXTERIOR: DEATH STAR TRENCH

The Rebel fighters evade the Imperial laser blasts.

INTERIOR: RED TEN'S COCKPIT

Red Ten looks around for the Imperial fighters.
RED TEN: We should be able to see it by now.

EXTERIOR: DEATH STAR TRENCH

From the cockpits of the Rebel pilots, the surface of the Death Star streaks by, with Imperial laserfire shooting toward them.

INTERIOR: RED LEADER'S COCKPIT

RED LEADER: Keep your eyes open for those fighters!

INTERIOR: RED TEN'S COCKPIT

RED TEN: There's too much interference!

EXTERIOR: SPACE—DEATH STAR TRENCH

Three X-wing fighters move in formation down the Death Star trench.

RED TEN'S VOICE: Red Five, can you see them from where you are?

INTERIOR: LUKE'S X-WING FIGHTER—COCKPIT

Luke looks down at the Death Star surface below.
LUKE: No sign of any...wait!

INTERIOR: RED TEN'S COCKPIT

Red Ten looks up and sees the Imperial fighters.
LUKE: (over headset) Coming in point three five.
RED TEN: I see them.

EXTERIOR: SURFACE OF THE DEATH STAR

Three TIE fighters, Vader flanked by two wingmen, dive in a tight formation. The sun reflects off their dominate

solar fins as they loop toward the Death Star's surface.
INTERIOR: RED LEADER'S COCKPIT

Above: Storyboard, Alex Tavoularis

Red Leader pulls his targeting device in front of his eyes and makes several adjustments.
RED LEADER: I'm in range.

EXTERIOR: SURFACE OF THE DEATH STAR

Red Leader's X-wing moves up the Death Star trench.

INTERIOR: RED LEADER'S COCKPIT

RED LEADER: Target's coming up!
Red Leader looks at his computer target readout screen. He then looks into his targeting device.
RED LEADER: Just hold them off for a few seconds.

INTERIOR: DARTH VADER'S COCKPIT

Vader adjusts his control lever and dives on the X-wing fighters.
VADER: Close up formation.

INTERIOR: DEATH STAR TRENCH

The three TIE fighters move in formation across the Death Star surface.

INTERIOR: RED LEADER'S COCKPIT

RED LEADER: Almost there!
Red Leader lines up his target on the targeting device cross hairs.

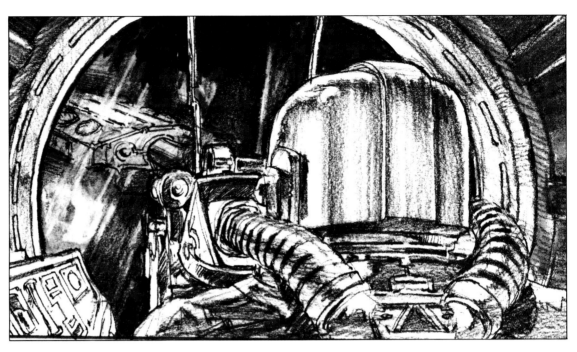

Right: Storyboard, Alex Tavoularis

EXTERIOR: SURFACE OF THE DEATH STAR

Vader and his wingman zoom down the trench.

INTERIOR: DARTH VADER'S COCKPIT

Vader rapidly approaches the two X-wings of Red Ten and Red Twelve. Vader's laser cannon flashes below the view of the front porthole. The X-wings show in the center of Vader's computer screen.

EXTERIOR: SPACE

Red Twelve's X-wing fighter is hit by Vader's laserfire, and it explodes into flames against the trench.

INTERIOR: RED TEN'S COCKPIT

Red Ten works at his controls furiously, trying to avoid Vader's fighter behind him.
RED TEN: You'd better let her loose.

INTERIOR: RED LEADER'S COCKPIT

Red Leader is concentrating on his targeting device.
RED LEADER: Almost there!

INTERIOR: RED TEN'S COCKPIT

Red Ten panics.
RED TEN: I can't hold them!

EXTERIOR: SURFACE OF THE DEATH STAR

Vader and his wingmen whip through the trench in pursuit of the Rebel fighters.

INTERIOR: DARTH VADER'S COCKPIT

Vader cooly pushes the fire button on his control stick.

INTERIOR: RED TEN'S COCKPIT

Darth Vader's well-aimed laserfire proves to be unavoidable, and strikes Red Ten's ship. Red Ten screams in anguish and pain.

EXTERIOR: SPACE AROUND THE DEATH STAR

Red Ten's ship explodes and bursts into flames.

INTERIOR: RED LEADER'S COCKPIT

Grimly, Red Leader takes careful aim and watches his computer targeting device, which shows the target lined up in the cross hairs, and fires.

INTERIOR: RED LEADER'S COCKPIT
RED LEADER: It's away!

EXTERIOR: DEATH STAR SURFACE

Red Leader's X-wing pulls up just before a huge explosion billows out of the trench.

INTERIOR: DEATH STAR

An armed Imperial stormtrooper is knocked to the floor from the attack explosion. Other troopers scurrying about the corridors are knocked against the wall and lose their balance.

INTERIOR: MASSASSI OUTPOST—WAR ROOM

Leia and the others stare at the computer screen.
RED NINE'S VOICE: (over speaker) It's a hit!
RED LEADER: (over speaker) Negative.

INTERIOR: RED LEADER'S COCKPIT

Red Leader looks back at the receding Death Star. Tiny explosions are visible in the distance.
RED LEADER: Negative! It didn't go in. It just impacted on the surface.

EXTERIOR: SPACE AROUND THE DEATH STAR—TIE FIGHTER

Darth Vader peels off in pursuit as Red Leader's X-wing passes the Death Star horizon.

INTERIOR: DARTH VADER'S COCKPIT

Left: Production painting, Ralph McQuarrie; above and below: sketches of X-wing fighter in Death Star trench, Ralph McQuarrie

Vader swings his ship around for his next kill.

INTERIOR: RED LEADER'S COCKPIT

LUKE: (over headset) Red Leader, we're right above you. Turn to point...

INTERIOR: LUKE'S X-WING FIGHTER—COCKPIT

Luke tries to spot Red Leader. He looks down at the Death Star surface.
LUKE: ...oh-five; we'll cover for you.
RED LEADER (over headset) Stay there...

INTERIOR: RED LEADER'S COCKPIT

A wary Red Leader looks about nervously.
RED LEADER: ...I just lost my starboard engine.

INTERIOR: LUKE'S X-WING FIGHTER—COCKPIT

Luke looks excitedly toward Red Leader's X-wing.
RED LEADER: (over headset) Get set up for your attack run.

INTERIOR: DARTH VADER'S COCKPIT

Vader's gloved hands make contact with the control sticks, and he presses their firing buttons.

INTERIOR: RED LEADER'S COCKPIT

Red Leader fights to gain control of his ship.

EXTERIOR: SPACE AROUND THE DEATH STAR

Laserbolts are flung from Vader's TIE fighter, connecting with Red Leader's Rebel X-wing fighter. Red Leader buys it, creating a tremendous explosion far below. He screams and is destroyed.

INTERIOR: LUKE'S X-WING FIGHTER—COCKPIT

Luke looks out the window of his X-wing at the explosion far below. For the first time, he feels the helplessness of his situation.

INTERIOR: DEATH STAR

Grand Moff Tarkin casts a sinister eye at the computer screen.
DEATH STAR INTERCOM VOICE: Rebel base, one minute and closing.

INTERIOR: MASSASSI OUTPOST—WAR ROOM

Dodonna and Princess Leia, with Threepio beside them, listen intently to the talk between the pilots. The room is grim after Red Leader's death. Princess Leia nervously paces the room.
LUKE: (over speaker) Biggs, Wedge, let's close it up. We're going in. We're going in full throttle.

INTERIOR: WEDGE'S COCKPIT

The horizon twists as Wedge begins to pull out.
WEDGE: Right with you, boss.

EXTERIOR: SPACE AROUND THE DEATH STAR

The two X-wings peel off against a background of stars and dive toward the Death Star.

INTERIOR: BIGGS'S COCKPIT

BIGGS: Luke, at that speed will you be able to pull out in time?

INTERIOR: LUKE'S X-WING FIGHTER—COCKPIT

LUKE: It'll be just like Beggar's Canyon back home.

EXTERIOR: SPACE AROUND THE DEATH STAR

The three X-wings move in, unleashing a barrage of laserfire. Laserbolts are returned from the Death Star.

INTERIOR: BIGGS'S COCKPIT

Luke's lifelong friend struggles with his controls.
BIGGS: We'll stay back far enough to cover you.

INTERIOR: LUKE'S COCKPIT

Flak and laserbolts flash outside Luke's cockpit window.
WEDGE: (over headset) My scope shows the tower, but I can't see the exhaust port! Are you sure the computer can hit it?

EXTERIOR: DEATH STAR—GUN EMPLACEMENT

The Death Star laser cannon slowly rotates as it shoots laserbolts.

INTERIOR: LUKE'S X-WING FIGHTER—COCKPIT

Luke looks around for the Imperial TIE fighters. He thinks for a moment and then moves his targeting device into position.
LUKE: Watch yourself! Increase speed full throttle!

returned, knicking one of his wings close to the engine.
LUKE: (to Artoo) Artoo...that, that stabilizer's broken loose again! See if you can't lock it down!

EXTERIOR: LUKE'S X-WING FIGHTER

Artoo works to repair the damages. The canyon wall rushes by in the background, making his delicate task seem even more precarious.

EXTERIOR: DEATH STAR

Two laser cannons are firing on the Rebel fighters.

INTERIOR: WEDGE'S COCKPIT

Wedge looks up and sees the TIE ships.

Sketches: Joe Johnston

DEATH STAR OVER LASER EYE

INTERIOR: WEDGE'S COCKPIT

Wedge looks excitedly about for any sign of the TIE fighters.
WEDGE: What about that tower?

INTERIOR: LUKE'S X-WING FIGHTER—COCKPIT

LUKE: You worry about those fighters! I'll worry about the tower!

EXTERIOR: DEATH STAR SURFACE

Luke's X-wing streaks through the trench, firing lasers.

INTERIOR: LUKE'S X-WING FIGHTER—COCKPIT

Luke breaks into a nervous sweat as the laserfire is

INTERIOR: LUKE'S X-WING FIGHTER—COCKPIT

Luke's targeting device marks off the distance to the target.

EXTERIOR: SPACE AROUND THE DEATH STAR

Vader and his wingmen zoom closer.

INTERIOR: DARTH VADER'S COCKPIT

Vader adjusts his controls and fires laserbolts at two X-wings flying down the trench. He scores a direct hit on Wedge.

INTERIOR: MASSASSI OUTPOST—WAR ROOM

Leia and the others are grouped around the computer board.
WEDGE: (over speaker) I'm hit! I can't stay with you.
LUKE: (over speaker) Get clear, Wedge.

INTERIOR: LUKE'S X-WING FIGHTER—COCKPIT
LUKE: You can't do any more good back there!

INTERIOR: WEDGE'S COCKPIT
WEDGE: Sorry!

EXTERIOR: SPACE AROUND THE DEATH STAR
Wedge pulls his crippled X-wing back away from the battle.

EXTERIOR: SPACE AROUND THE DEATH STAR
The three TIE fighters move ever closer, closing in on Luke and Biggs.

INTERIOR: LUKE'S X-WING FIGHTER—COCKPIT
Luke looks back anxiously at little Artoo.
LUKE: Artoo, try and increase the power!

EXTERIOR: LUKE'S X-WING FIGHTER
Ignoring the bumpy ride, flak, and lasers, a beeping Artoo-Detoo struggles to increase the power, his dome turning from side to side.

EXTERIOR: SPACE AROUND THE DEATH STAR

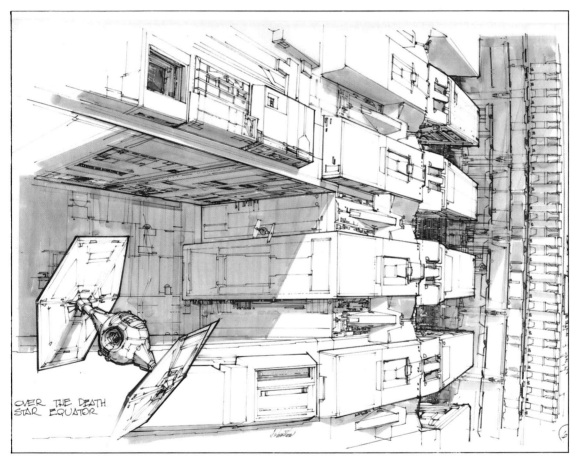

OVER THE DEATH STAR EQUATOR

INTERIOR: DARTH VADER'S COCKPIT
Vader watches the escape but issues a command to his wingmen.
VADER: Let him go! Stay on the leader!

EXTERIOR: SPACE AROUND THE DEATH STAR
Luke's X-wing speeds down the trench; the three TIE fighters, still in perfect unbroken formation, tail close behind.

INTERIOR: BIGGS'S COCKPIT
Biggs looks around at the TIE fighters. He is worried.
BIGGS: Hurry, Luke, they're coming in much faster this time. I can't hold them!

Stealthily, the TIE formation creeps closer.

INTERIOR: DARTH VADER'S COCKPIT
Vader adjusts his control stick.

INTERIOR: BIGGS'S COCKPIT
Biggs looks around at the TIE fighters.

INTERIOR: LUKE'S X-WING FIGHTER—COCKPIT
Luke looks into his targeting device. He moves it away for a moment and ponders its use. He looks back into the computer targeter.
BIGGS: (over headset) Hurry up, Luke!

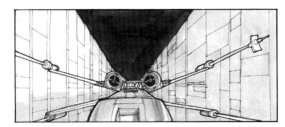

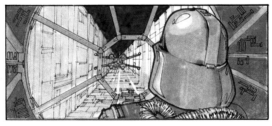

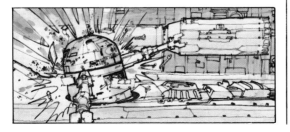

Storyboards: Gary Myers,
Paul Huston, Steve Gawley,
Ronnie Shepherd; under
direction of Joe Johnston

EXTERIOR: SPACE AROUND THE DEATH STAR

Vader and his wingmen race through the Death Star trench. Biggs moves in to cover for Luke, but Vader gains on him.

INTERIOR: BIGGS'S COCKPIT

Biggs sees the TIE fighters aiming at him.
BIGGS: Wait!

INTERIOR: DARTH VADER'S COCKPIT

Vader squeezes the fire button on his controls.

INTERIOR: BIGGS'S COCKPIT

Biggs' cockpit explodes around him, lighting him in red.

EXTERIOR: SURFACE OF THE DEATH STAR

Biggs' ship bursts into a million flaming bits and scatters across the surface.

INTERIOR: MASSASSI OUTPOST—WAR ROOM

Leia and the others stare at the computer board.

INTERIOR: LUKE'S X-WING COCKPIT

Luke is stunned by Biggs' death. His eyes are watering, but his anger is also growing.

INTERIOR: DEATH STAR—CONTROL ROOM

Grand Moff Tarkin watches the projected target screen with satisfaction.
DEATH STAR INTERCOM VOICE: Rebel base, thirty seconds and closing.

INTERIOR: DARTH VADER'S COCKPIT

Vader takes aim on Luke and talks to his wingman.
VADER: I'm on the leader.

EXTERIOR: SURFACE OF THE DEATH STAR—LUKE'S SHIP

Luke's ship streaks through the trench of the Death Star.

INTERIOR: MASSASSI OUTPOST—WAR ROOM

Princess Leia returns her general's worried and doubtful glances with a solid, grim determination. Threepio seems nervous.
THREEPIO: Hang on, Artoo!

INTERIOR: LUKE'S X-WING—COCKPIT

Luke concentrates on his targeting device.

EXTERIOR: SURFACE OF THE DEATH STAR

Three TIE fighters charge away down the trench toward Luke.

INTERIOR: DARTH VADER'S COCKPIT

Vader's fighters curl around the control stick.

INTERIOR: LUKE'S X-WING—COCKPIT

Luke adjusts the lens of his targeting device.

EXTERIOR: SURFACE OF THE DEATH STAR

Luke's ship charges down the trench.

INTERIOR: LUKE'S X-WING—COCKPIT

Luke lines up the yellow cross-hair lines of the targeting device's screen. He looks into the targeting device, then starts at a voice he hears.
BEN'S VOICE: Use the Force, Luke.

EXTERIOR: SURFACE OF THE DEATH STAR

The Death Star trench zooms by.

INTERIOR: LUKE'S X-WING—COCKPIT

Luke looks up, then starts to look back into the targeting device. He has second thoughts.
BEN'S VOICE: Let go, Luke.
   A grim determination sweeps across Luke's face as he closes his eyes and starts to mumble Ben's training to himself.

EXTERIOR: SURFACE OF THE DEATH STAR

Luke's fighter streaks through the trench.

INTERIOR: DARTH VADER'S COCKPIT

VADER: The Force is strong with this one!

EXTERIOR: SURFACE OF THE DEATH STAR

Vader follows Luke's X-wing down the trench.

INTERIOR: LUKE'S X-WING—COCKPIT

Luke looks to the targeting device, then away as he hears Ben's voice.
BEN'S VOICE: Luke, trust me.
   Luke's hand reaches for the control panel and presses the button. The targeting device moves away.

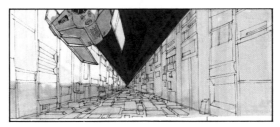

INTERIOR: MASSASSI OUTPOST—WAR ROOM

Leia and the others stand watching the projected screen.
BASE VOICE: (over speaker) His computer's off. Luke, you switched off your targeting computer. What's wrong?
LUKE: (over speaker) Nothing. I'm all right.

EXTERIOR: SURFACE OF THE DEATH STAR

Luke's ship streaks ever closer to the exhaust port.

INTERIOR: LUKE'S X-WING—COCKPIT

Luke looks at the Death Star surface streaking by.

EXTERIOR: LUKE'S X-WING-FIGHTER

Artoo-Detoo turns his head from side to side, beeping in anticipation.

EXTERIOR: SURFACE OF THE DEATH STAR

The three TIE fighters, manned by Vader and his two wingmen, follow Luke's X-wing down the trench.

INTERIOR: DARTH VADER'S COCKPIT

Vader maneuvers his controls as he looks at his doomed target. He presses the fire buttons on his control sticks. Laserfire shoots toward Luke's X-wing fighter.

EXTERIOR: LUKE'S X-WING FIGHTER

A large burst of Vader's laserfire engulfs Artoo. The arms

Right and opposite page:
Sketches of Rebel ceremony set,
Ralph McQuarrie

go limp on the smoking little droid as he makes a high-pitched sound.

INTERIOR: LUKE'S X-WING FIGHTER—COCKPIT

Luke looks frantically back over his shoulder at Artoo.

EXTERIOR: LUKE'S X-WING FIGHTER

Smoke billows out around little Artoo and sparks begin to fly.
LUKE: I've lost Artoo!
  Artoo's beeping sounds die out.

INTERIOR: MASSASSI OUTPOST—WAR ROOM

Leia and the others stare intently at the projected screen, while Threepio watches the Princess. Lights representing the Death Star and targets glow brightly.
MASSASSI INTERCOM VOICE: The Death Star has cleared the planet. The Death Star has cleared the planet.

INTERIOR: DEATH STAR—CONTROL ROOM

Tarkin glares at the projected target screen.
DEATH STAR INTERCOM VOICE: Rebel base, in range.
TARKIN: You may fire when ready.
DEATH STAR INTERCOM VOICE: Commence primary ignition.

An officer reaches up and pushes buttons on the control panel, as green lighted buttons turn to red.

EXTERIOR: SURFACE OF THE DEATH STAR

The three TIE fighters zoom down the Death Star trench in pursuit of Luke, never breaking formation.

INTERIOR: LUKE'S COCKPIT

Luke looks anxiously at the exhaust port.

INTERIOR: DARTH VADER'S COCKPIT

Vader adjusts his control sticks, checking his projected targeting screen.

EXTERIOR: SURFACE OF THE DEATH STAR

Luke's ship barrels down the trench.

INTERIOR: DARTH VADER'S COCKPIT

Vader's targeting computer swings around into position. Vader takes careful aim on Luke's X-wing fighter.
VADER: I have you now.
  He pushes the fire buttons.

EXTERIOR: SURFACE OF THE DEATH STAR

The three TIE fighters move in on Luke. As Vader's center

fighter unleashes a volley of laserfire, one of the TIE ships at his side is hit and explodes into flame. The two remaining ships continue to move in.

INTERIOR: LUKE'S X-WING FIGHTER—COCKPIT

Luke looks about, wondering whose laserfire destroyed Vader's wingman.

INTERIOR: DARTH VADER'S COCKPIT

Vader is taken by surprise, and looks out from his cockpit.
VADER: What?

INTERIOR: DARTH VADER'S WINGMAN—COCKPIT

Vader's wingman searches around him trying to locate the unknown attacker.

INTERIOR: MILLENNIUM FALCON—COCKPIT

Han and Chewbacca grin from ear to ear.
HAN: (yelling) Yahoo!

EXTERIOR: SPACE AROUND THE DEATH STAR

The Millennium Falcon heads right at the two TIE fighters. It's a collision course.

INTERIOR: WINGMAN'S COCKPIT

The wingman spots the pirateship coming at him and warns the Dark Lord.
WINGMAN: Look out!

EXTERIOR: DEATH STAR TRENCH

Vader's wingman panics at the sight of the oncoming pirate starship and veers radically to one side, colliding with Vader's TIE fighter in the process. Vader's wingman crashes into the side wall of the trench and explodes. Vader's damaged ship spins out of the trench with a damaged wing.

EXTERIOR: SPACE AROUND THE DEATH STAR

Vader's ship spins out of control with a bent solar fin, heading for deep space.

INTERIOR: DARTH VADER'S COCKPIT

Vader turns round and round in circles as his ship spins into space.

EXTERIOR: SURFACE OF THE DEATH STAR

Solo's ship moves in toward the Death Star trench.

INTERIOR: MILLENNIUM FALCON—COCKPIT

Solo, smiling, speaks to Luke over his headset mike.

HAN: (into mike) You're all clear, kid.

INTERIOR: MASSASSI OUTPOST—WAR ROOM

Leia and the others listen to Solo's transmission.
HAN: (over speaker) Now let's blow this thing and go home!

INTERIOR: LUKE'S X-WING FIGHTER—COCKPIT

Luke looks up and smiles. He concentrates on the exhaust port, then fires his laser torpedoes.

EXTERIOR: SURFACE OF THE DEATH STAR

Luke's torpedo shoots toward the port and seems to simply disappear into the surface and not explode. But the shots do find their mark and have gone into the exhaust port and are heading for the main reactor.

INTERIOR: LUKE'S X-WING FIGHTER—COCKPIT

Luke throws his head back in relief.

INTERIOR: DEATH STAR

An Imperial soldier runs to the control panel board and pulls the attack lever as the board behind him lights up.
INTERCOM VOICE: Stand by to fire at Rebel base.

EXTERIOR: SPACE AROUND THE DEATH STAR

Two X-wings, a Y-wing, and the pirateship race toward Yavin in the distance.

INTERIOR: DEATH STAR

Several Imperial soldiers, flanking a pensive Grand Moff Tarkin, busily push control levers and buttons.
INTERCOM VOICE: Standing by.
The rumble of a distant explosion begins.

EXTERIOR: SPACE AROUND THE DEATH STAR

The Rebel ships race out of sight, leaving the moon-like Death Star alone against a blanket of stars. Several small flashes appear on the surface. The Death Star bursts into a supernova, creating a spectacular heavenly display.

INTERIOR: MILLENNIUM FALCON—COCKPIT

HAN: Great shot, kid. That was one in a million.

INTERIOR: LUKE'S X-WING FIGHTER—COCKPIT

Luke is at last at ease, and his eyes are closed.
BEN'S VOICE: Remember, the Force will be with you...always.
The ship rocks back and forth.

EXTERIOR: DARTH VADER'S TIE FIGHTER

Vader's ship spins off into space.

Matte paintings for Rebel ceremony : Peter Ellenshaw

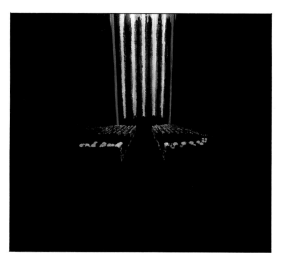

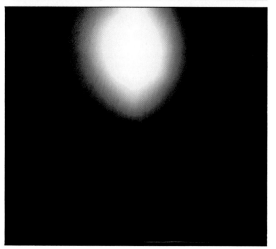

EXTERIOR: SPACE

The Rebel ships race toward the fourth moon of Yavin.

INTERIOR: MASSASSI OUTPOST—MAIN HANGAR

Luke climbs out of his starship fighter and is cheered by a throng of ground crew and pilots. Luke climbs down the ladder as they all welcome him with laughter, cheers, and shouting.

Princess Leia rushes toward him.

LEIA: Luke! Luke! Luke!

She throws her arms around Luke and hugs him as they dance around a circle. Solo runs in toward Luke and they embrace one another, slapping each other on the back.

HAN: (laughing) Hey! Hey!

LUKE: (laughing) I knew you'd come back! I just knew it!

HAN: Well, I wasn't gonna let you get all the credit and take all the reward.

Luke and Han look at one another, as Solo playfully shoves at Luke's face. Leia moves in between them.

LEIA: (laughing) Hey, I knew there was more to you than money.

Luke looks toward the ship.

LUKE: Oh, no!

The fried little Artoo-Detoo is lifted off the back of the fighter and carried off under the worried eyes of Threepio.

THREEPIO: Oh, my! Artoo! Can you hear me? Say something! (to mechanic) You can repair him, can't you?

TECHNICIAN: We'll get to work on him right away.

THREEPIO: You must repair him! Sir, if any of my circuits or gears will help, I'll gladly donate them.

LUKE: He'll be all right.

INTERIOR: MASSASSI OUTPOST—MAIN THRONE ROOM

Luke, Han, and Chewbacca enter the huge ruins of the main temple. Hundreds of troops are lined up in neat rows. Banners are flying and at the far end stands a vision in white, the beautiful young Senator Leia. Luke and the others solemnly march up the long aisle and kneel before Senator Leia. From one side of the temple marches a shined-up and fully repaired Artoo-Detoo. He waddles up to the group and stands next to an equally pristine Threepio, who is rather awestruck by the whole event. Chewbacca is confused. Dodonna and several other dignitaries sit on the left of the Princess Leia. Leia is dressed in a long white dress and is staggeringly beautiful. She rises and places a gold medallion around Han's neck. He winks at her. She then repeats the ceremony with Luke, who is moved by the event. They turn and face the assembled troops, who all bow before them. Chewbacca growls and Artoo beeps with happiness.

FADE OUT

END CREDITS OVER STARS

THE END

Above: Costume sketch for Rebel ceremony, John Mollo; left: production painting, Ralph McQuarrie

CREDITS

Written and Directed by
GEORGE LUCAS
Produced by
GARY KURTZ

STARRING
MARK HAMILL   HARRISON FORD   CARRIE FISHER
PETER CUSHING
and ALEC GUINNESS
with
ANTHONY DANIELS, KENNY BAKER, PETER MAYHEW,
DAVID PROWSE, JACK PURVIS, EDDIE BYRNE

Production Designer
JOHN BARRY
Director of Photography
GILBERT TAYLOR, B.S.C.
Music by
JOHN WILLIAMS
Performed by The London Symphony Orchestra; Original Music
Copyright 1977 © by Fox Fanfare Music, Inc.
Special Photographic Effects Supervisor
JOHN DYKSTRA
Special Production and Mechanical Effects Supervisor
JOHN STEARS
Film Editors
PAUL HIRSCH, MARCIA LUCAS, RICHARD CHEW
Production Supervisor
ROBERT WATTS
Production Illustration
RALPH McQUARRIE
Costume Designer
JOHN MOLLO
Art Directors
NORMAN REYNOLDS, LESLIE DILLEY
Make up Supervisor
STUART FREEBORN
Production Sound Mixer
DEREK BALL
Casting
IRENE LAMB, DIANE CRITTENDEN, VIC RAMOS
Supervising Sound Editor
SAM SHAW
Special Dialogue and Sound Effects
BEN BURTT
Sound Editors
ROBERT R. RUTLEDGE, GORDON DAVIDSON,
GENE CORSO
Supervising Music Editor
KENNETH WANNBERG
Rerecording Mixers
DON MacDOUGALL, BOB MINKLER, RAY WEST,
ROBERT LITT, MIKE MINKLER, LESTER FRESHOLTZ,
RICHARD PORTMAN
Dolby Sound Consultant
STEPHEN KATZ
Orchestrations
HERBERT W. SPENCER
Music Scoring Mixer
ERIC TOMLINSON

Assistant Film Editors
TODD BOEKELHEIDE, JAY MIRACLE,
COLIN KITCHENS, BONNIE KOEHLER
Camera Operators
RONNIE TAYLOR, GEOFF GLOVER
Set Decorator
ROGER CHRISTIAN
Production Manager
BRUCE SHARMAN
Assistant Directors
TONY WAYE, GERRY GAVIGAN, TERRY MADDEN
Location Manager
ARNOLD ROSS
Assistant to Producer
BUNNY ALSUP
Assistant to Director
LUCY AUTREY WILSON
Production Assistants
PAT CARR, MIKI HERMAN
Gaffer
RON TABERA
Property Master
FRANK BRUTON
Wardrobe Supervisor
RON BECK
Stunt Coordinator
PETER DIAMOND
Continuity
ANN SKINNER
Titles
DAN PERRI
Second Unit Photography
CARROLL BALLARD, RICK CLEMENTE,
ROBERT DALVA, TAK FUJIMOTO
Second Unit Art Direction
LEON ERICKSON, AL LOCATELLI
Second Unit Production Managers
DAVID LESTER, PETER HERALD, PEPI LENZI
Second Unit Make-up
RICK BAKER, DOUGLAS BESWICK
Assistant Sound Editors
ROXANNE JONES, KAREN SHARP
Production Controller
BRIAN GIBBS
Location Auditor
RALPH M. LEO
Assistant Auditors
STEVE CULLIP, PENNY McCARTHY, KIM FALKINBURG
Advertising/Publicity Supervisor
CHARLES LIPPINCOTT
Unit Publicist
BRIAN DOYLE
Still Photographer
JOHN JAY

MINIATURE AND OPTICAL EFFECTS UNIT
First Cameraman
RICHARD EDLUND
Second Cameraman
DENNIS MUREN

Assistant Camermen
DOUGLAS SMITH, KENNETH RALSTON, DAVID ROBMAN
Second Unit Photography
BRUCE LOGAN
Composite Optical Photography
ROBERT BLALACK (PRAXIS)
Optical Photography Coordinator
PAUL ROTH
Optical Printer Operators
DAVID BERRY, DAVID McCUE, RICHARD PECORELLA,
ELDON RICKMAN, JAMES VAN TREES, JR.
Optical Camera Assistants
CALEB ASCHKYNAZO, JOHN C. MOULDS,
BRUCE NICHOLSON,
GARY SMITH, BERT TERRERI,
DONNA TRACY, JIM WELLS, VICKY WITT
Production Supervisor
GEORGE E. MATHER
Matte Artist
P. S. ELLENSHAW
Planet and Satellite Artist
RALPH McQUARRIE
Effects Illustration and Design
JOSEPH JOHNSTON
Additional Spacecraft Design
COLIN CANTWELL
Chief Model Maker
GRANT McCUNE
Model Builders
DAVID BEASLEY, JON ERLAND, LORNE PETERSON,
STEVE GAWLEY, PAUL HUSTON, DAVID JONES
Animation and Rotoscope Design
ADAM BECKETT
Animators
MICHAEL ROSS, PETER KURAN, JONATHAN SEAY,
CHRIS CASADY, LYN GERRY, DIANA WILSON
Stop Motion Animation
JON BERG, PHIL TIPPETT
Miniature Explosions
JOE VISKOCIL, GREG AUER
Computer Animation and Graphic Displays
DAN O'BANNON, LARRY CUBA, JOHN WASH,
JAY TEITZELL, IMAGE WEST
Film Control Coordinator
MARY M. LIND
Film Librarians
CINDY ISMAN, CONNIE McCRUM, PAMELA MALOUF
Electronics Design
ALVAH J. MILLER
Special Components
JAMES SHOURT
Assistants,
MASAAKI NORIHORO, ELEANOR PORTER
Camera and Mechanical Design
DON TRUMBULL, RICHARD ALEXANDER,
WILLIAM SHOURT
Special Mechanical Equipment
JERRY GREENWOOD, DOUGLAS BARNETT, STUART ZIFF,
DAVID SCOTT
Production Managers
BOB SHEPHERD, LON TINNEY

Production Staff
PATRICIA ROSE DUIGNAN, MARK KLINE,
RHONDA PECK, RON NATHAN
Assistant Editor (Opticals)
BRUCE MICHAEL GREEN
Additional Optical Effects
VAN DER VEER PHOTO EFFECTS,
RAY MERCER & COMPANY,
MODERN FILM EFFECTS,
MASTER FILM EFFECTS
DE PATIE-FRELENG ENTERPRISES, INC.

PANAVISION® TECHNICOLOR® Prints by DELUXE®
Making Films Sound Better, DOLBY SYSTEM®
Noise Reduction—High Fidelity

CAST

Luke Skywalker	MARK HAMILL
Han Solo	HARRISON FORD
Princess Leia Organa	CARRIE FISHER
Grand Moff Tarkin	PETER CUSHING
Ben (Obi-Wan) Kenobi	ALEC GUINNESS
See Threepio (C-3PO)	ANTHONY DANIELS
Artoo-Detoo (R2-D2)	KENNY BAKER
Chewbacca	PETER MAYHEW
Lord Darth Vader	DAVID PROWSE
Uncle Owen	PHIL BROWN
Aunt Beru	SHELAGH FRASER
Chief Jawa	JACK PURVIS
General Dodonna	ALEX McCRINDLE
General Willard	EDDIE BYRNE
Red Leader	DREWE HEMLEY
Red Two (Wedge)	DENNIS LAWSON
Red Three (Biggs)	GARRICK HAGON
Red Four (John "D")	JACK KLAFF
Red Six (Porkins)	WILLIAM HOOTKINS
Gold Leader	ANGUS McINNIS
Gold Two	JEREMY SINDEN
Gold Five	GRAHAM ASHLEY
General Taggi	DON HENDERSON
General Motti	RICHARD LE PARMENTIER
Commander One	LESLIE SCHOFIELD

Photographed in Tunisia
Tikal National Park, Guatemala
Death Valley National Monument, California
and at EMI Elstree Studios, Borehamwood, England
Music Recorded at Anvil Recording Studios, Denham, England
Post Production Completed at American Zoetrope, San Francisco, California
Rerecording at Samuel Goldwyn Studios, Los Angeles, California

The producers wish to thank the government of Tunisia, the Institute of Anthropology and History of Guatemala, and the National Park Service, United States Department of the Interior, for their cooperation.

Copyright © 1977 by Twentieth Century-Fox Film Corporation

A LUCASFILM LTD. PRODUCTION

SECTION TWO 2 POSTER ART

Posters adapted from
Tommy Jung's original illustration.

Sweden.

Spain: Illustration, Hildebrandt

France.

Japan: Illustration, Seito

Israel.

Norway.

Preceeding pages: Campaign
posters; illustration, Tommy Jung;
design, Smollen, Smith, and
Connolly; ©1977 Twentieth
Century-Fox Film Corporation.

Spain

Great Britain.

Hong Kong.

Foreign Posters: Illustration,
Cantrell.

143

Poster Concepts :
Dan Goozee; design, Tony
Seiniger and Associates, © 1977
Twentieth Century-Fox Film
Corporation.

Poster for 1978 summer re-release: Illustration, Charlie White III and Drew Struzan; design, Charlie White III and friends; art direction, Charlie White III, © 1978 Twentieth Century-Fox Film Corporation.

Above left: First teaser poster: design, Doyle, Dane and Bernbach, © 1976 Twentieth Century-Fox Film Corporation; above right: teaser poster; © 1977 Twentieth Century-Fox Film Corporation; below left: first anniversary poster; photographer, Weldon Anderson; design, Tony Seiniger and Associates, © 1978 Twentieth Century-Fox Film Corporation; below right: campaign poster, Japan.

Concert poster: Illustration, John Alvin; design, Suzy Rice-Lane, © 1978 Twentieth Century-Fox Film Corporation.

Poster concepts, John Berkey

Poster Concepts
Above left: Philippe
Druillet; above right: Star
Wars comic poster, 1976, Howard
Chaykin; below left: Jim Campbell;
below right: Wojtek Siudmak

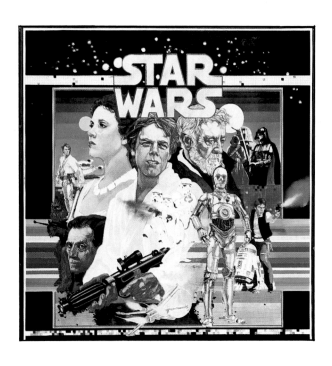

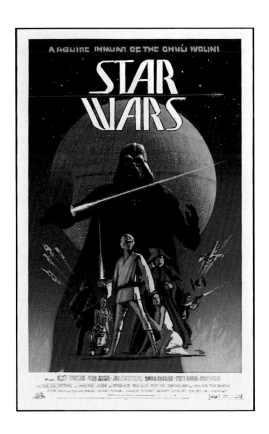

Poster Concepts:
Ralph McQuarrie;
below left: Star Wars Fan Club
poster: Ralph McQuarrie

SECTION THREE 3 SPIN-OFF CARTOONS AND FAN ART

DENNIS the MENACE

" IF THEY **DO** HAVE WARS, THEY'RE AWFUL QUIET ABOUT IT, JOEY. "

DENNIS THE MENACE Hank Ketcham © Field Enterprises

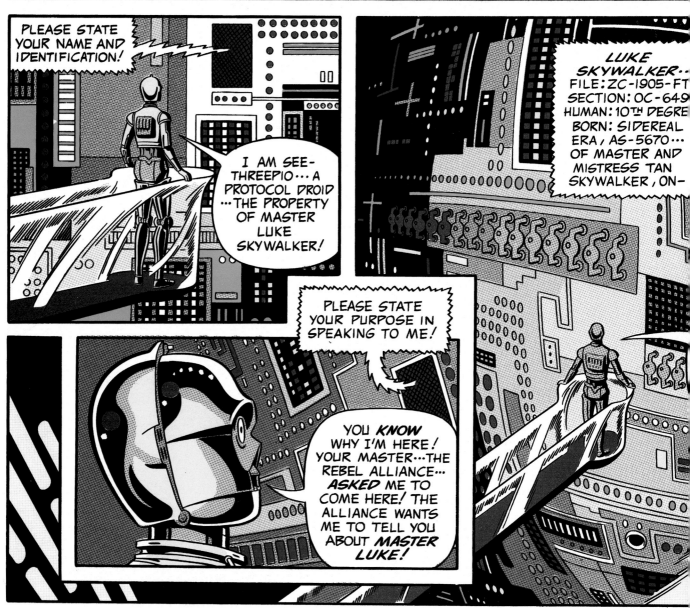

Sunday Comic Strip, Russ Manning, Los Angeles Times Syndicate, © 1979 Twentieth Century-Fox Film Corporation and Black Falcon, Ltd.

THIS IS AL MERTON AND I'M HERE ON THE U.S.-MEXICAN BORDER.

EACH DAY THOUSANDS OF ILLEGAL ALIENS CROSS HERE INTO THE U.S.

I THINK I SEE A COUPLE OF ALIENS NOW!

OH DEAR ARTOO-DETOO, ARE YOU SURE THIS IS THE RIGHT WAY?

BEEP BEEP WHRRRR

"May the Force be with you."

"I bought it! It's another spin-off thing from 'Star Wars'!"

Facing page: PLYMPTON, Bill
Plympton © 1977 Soho Weekly
News; left: editorial cartoon, Jeff
MacNelly, reprinted by permis-
sion of the Chicago Tribune-New
York News Syndicate, Inc.; above:
BERRY'S WORLD, Jim Berry,
reprinted by permission,
© 1977 NEA, Inc.

BERRY'S WORLD, Jim Berry, reprinted by permission,© 1977 NEA, Inc.

THE POOKAS, Paul Lowney and Anita Hodson. © Paul Lowney and Anita Hodson, L.A. Times Syndicate.

CROCK, Rechin, Parker and Wilder. © 1977 Field Enterprises, Inc. Courtesy of Field Newspaper Syndicate.

HI AND LOIS, Dik Browne. © 1978 King Features Syndicate, Inc.

Facing page, top left: Frank Interlandi, cartoonist, © 1977 Los Angeles Times, reprinted by permission; top right: THIS SPORTING LIFE, Forman and Templeton, reprinted by permission of the Chicago Tribune-New York Times Syndicate; below: editorial cartoon, Stayskal, reprinted by permission of the Chicago Tribune-New York News Syndicate.

Selected Covers, Marvel Comics

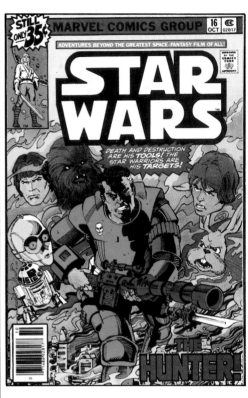

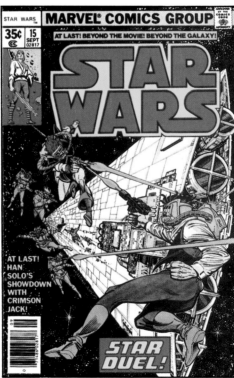

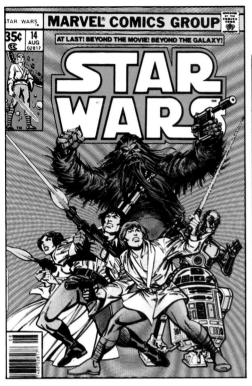

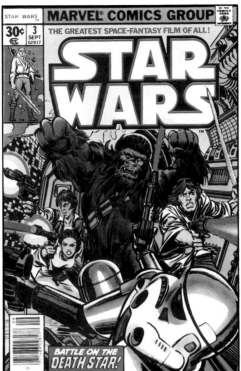

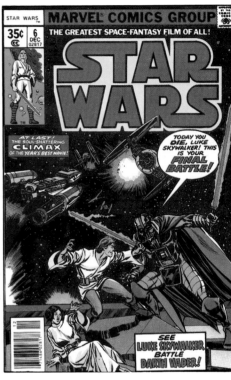

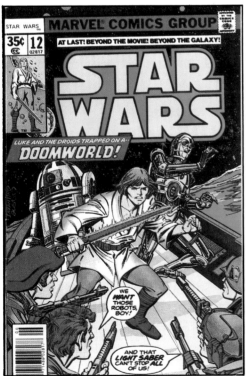

Below: Brian McGoldrick,
age 9

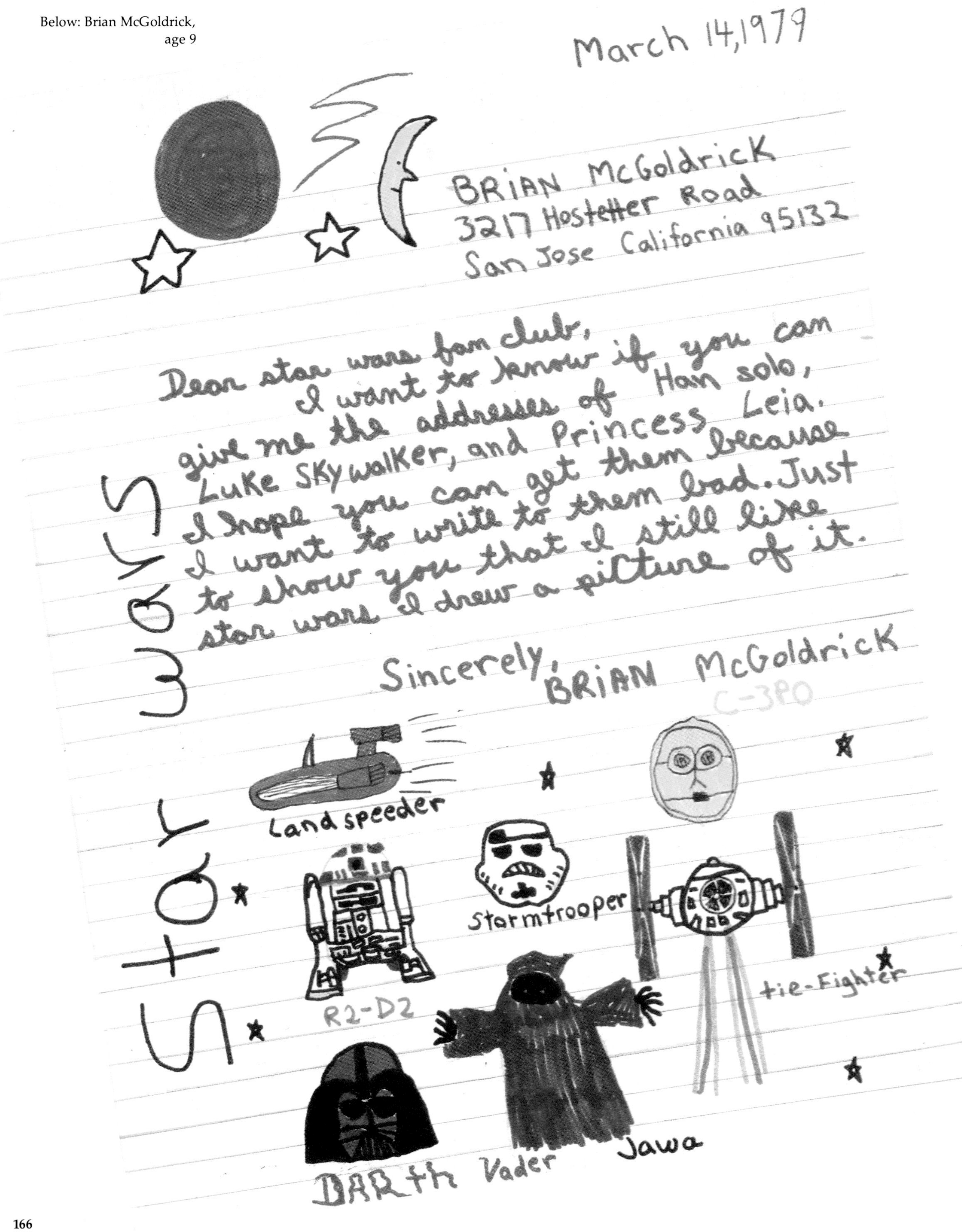

March 14, 1979

BRIAN McGoldrick
3217 Hostetter Road
San Jose California 95132

Dear star wars fan club,
I want to know if you can
give me the addresses of Han solo,
Luke Skywalker, and Princess Leia.
I hope you can get them because
I want to write to them bad. Just
to show you that I still like
star wars I drew a picture of it.

Sincerely, BRIAN McGoldrick

C-3PO

Land speeder

Stormtrooper

R2-D2

tie-Fighter

DARth Vader   Jawa

star wars

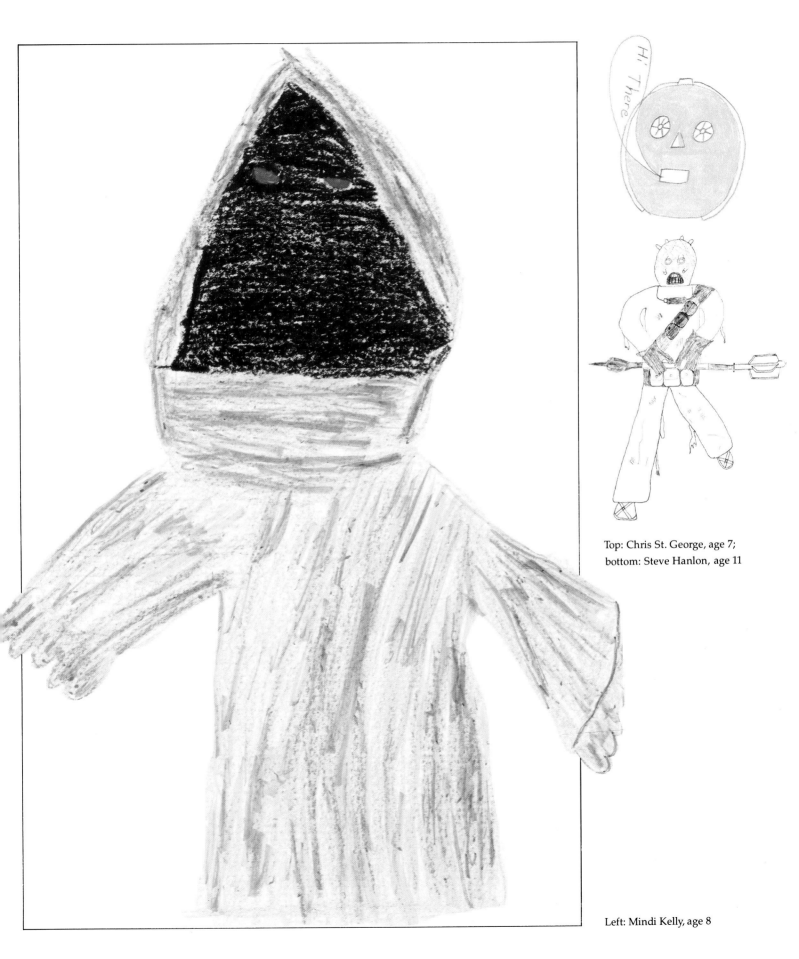

Top: Chris St. George, age 7;
bottom: Steve Hanlon, age 11

Left: Mindi Kelly, age 8

Opposite page:
Grant Ylitalo, age 11;
right: Michael Ahearn,
age 8; below:
Elizabeth Weber, age 9

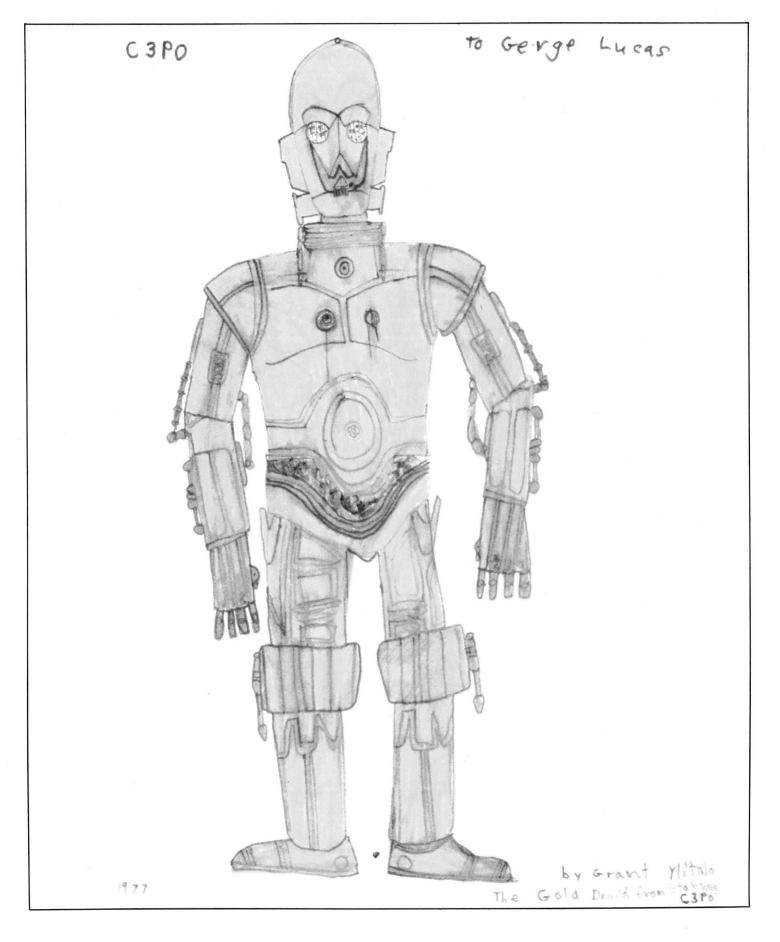

C3PO

to Gevrge Lucas

1977

by Grant Ylitalo
The Gold Droid from Star Wars
C3PO

Opposite page: Billy
Young, age 9; above:
Chris Stuvek, age 10;
below: Steve Mandich,
age 8

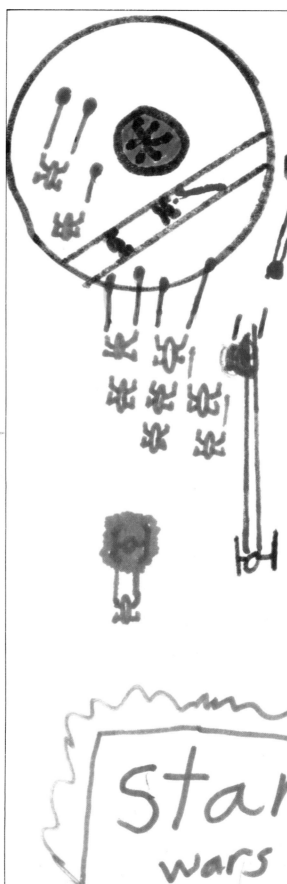

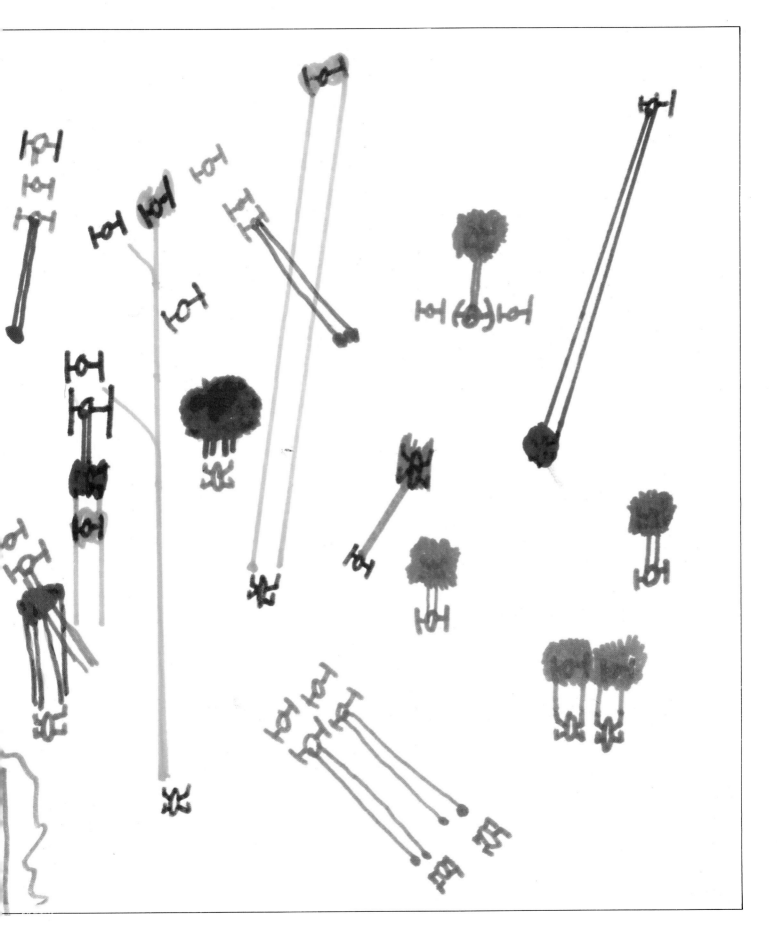

Above: Denise Fernandez, age 6; right: Amy Dian Lepisto, age 8; far right: Trey Fitz-Gerald, age 8; below: James Sladeck, age 11

Left: Louie Gaghan, age 7; below: Princess Leia, Richard Brian Davis, age 9; Han and Chewie, Tina Sales, age 8;

Below: Novero Potter, age 5

Left: Anne Olney, age 3 ;
far left: Cindy Frank, age 11

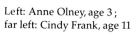